Beating the dragon

or before the last date stamped below.

2003

2007   1 4 DEC

15 FEB   2012

2007

Pearson Education

We work with leading authors to develop the
strongest educational materials in the social sciences,
bringing cutting-edge thinking and best learning
practice to a global market.

Under a range of well-known imprints, including
Prentice Hall, we craft high quality print and
electronic publications which help readers to understand
and apply their content, whether studying or at work.

To find out more about the complete range of our
publishing, please visit us on the World Wide Web at:
www.pearsoneduc.com

Beating the Dragon

THE RECOVERY FROM DEPENDENT DRUG USE

JAMES McINTOSH

Department of Social Policy and Social Work,
University of Glasgow.

NEIL McKEGANEY

Centre for Drug Misuse Research,
University of Glasgow.

Prentice
Hall

An imprint of **Pearson Education**

Harlow, England · London · New York · Reading, Massachusetts · San Francisco
Toronto · Don Mills, Ontario · Sydney · Tokyo · Singapore · Hong Kong · Seoul
Taipei · Cape Town · Madrid · Mexico City · Amsterdam · Munich · Paris · Milan

Pearson Education Limited
Edinburgh Gate
Harlow
Essex CM20 2JE

and Associated Companies throughout the world

Visit us on the World Wide Web at:
www.pearsoneduc.com

First published 2002

© Pearson Education Limited 2002

ISBN 0 130 87171 0

British Library Cataloguing-in-Publication Data
A catalogue record for this book is available from the British Library

Library of Congress Cataloging-in-Publication Data
McIntosh, James.
    Beating the dragon : the recovery from dependent drug use / James McIntosh,
Neil McKeganey.
        p. cm.
    Includes bibliographical references and index.
    ISBN 0–13–087171–0 (pbk.)
    1. Drug abuse—Psychological aspects. 2. Recovering addicts—Psychology.
3. Narcotic addicts—Rehabilitation—Psychological aspects. I. McKeganey,
Neil P. II. Title.

HV5801.M345   2001
362.29′18—dc21   2001021675

10 9 8 7 6 5 4 3 2 1
06 05 04 03 02

Typeset by 35 in 10/13pt Sabon

Contents

Acknowledgements

We would like to acknowledge our debt to the many individuals who agreed to be interviewed in our research and to talk in detail about what for many of them was an extraordinarily painful period in their lives. Quite simply, this book would not have been possible without their openness and their trust. In undertaking our research we were helped by a wide range of individuals. For assistance in interviewing we would like to acknowledge the contribution of Dr Gerda Reith, Mr Niall MacLean and Mr Ed Low. Evelyn Crombie and Carole Bain provided secretarial and clerical help for the project and Janis Neil undertook the task of formatting our manuscript. The research on which the book is based was funded by the Chief Scientist Office of the Scottish Executive. The views expressed within the book are those of the authors and should not be attributed to the funding body.

Dedications

FOR ISOBEL
Jim McIntosh

FOR REBECCA, GABRIEL AND DANIELLA-CLARE
Neil McKeganey

1 Introduction

This book is about how a group of 70 drug addicts were able to recover from their addiction to illegal drugs. It examines their reasons for deciding to give up drugs and explores the factors and circumstances which facilitated or impeded their attempts at recovery. Based on intensive interviews with the recovering addicts, the book presents the experience of coming off drugs from the perspective of the addicts themselves.

In the minds of many people drug addiction is assumed to be a one-way street from which there is no return. In reality, however, while drug addiction is associated with some of the worst and most frightening aspects of human experience, it is certainly not the case that there is no way back from it. The fact is that many addicts do eventually recover and this book is about how one group of addicts made this journey successfully. It is based upon the addicts' own accounts of their recovery: how they did it, what they had to do to overcome their dependence upon illegal drugs, what challenges they faced, how they overcame those challenges and in what ways their battle with their addiction was helped or hindered by other people.

We hope that this book will help to dispel a number of myths about drug users and drug addiction. First, we want to show that while drug addiction is an awful experience for the individuals concerned, and for all of those who are associated with them, there is a way back from it. An acceptance of the dictum 'once an addict always an addict' undermines, in a needlessly cynical way, the addicts' own efforts to recover and, as the book will show, the journey back from addiction is hard enough without the introduction of additional obstacles. Second, we hope the book shows that, in their struggle to recover from addiction, these individuals often demonstrate amazing strength, fortitude, openness, commitment and resilience. These are not qualities that are normally associated with drug addicts but they are here in abundance in the stories of their recovery. Third, we hope that the book conveys the sense that addicts are individuals in their own right. They are frequently presented in the media in caricature form as being weak-willed, threatening and immoral. The common image that is presented is that of a mindless, drug-crazed criminal and carrier of disease. While aspects of this portrayal are undoubtedly accurate – and, certainly, the participants in our own study would not deny that – there is another side to drug addiction that is seldom acknowledged or presented. What is missing from most descriptions of addiction is any sense of the addicts' individuality or of their ability to reflect upon their predicament. However, as we will see, the individuality of our interviewees can be clearly seen in the variety of their experiences and in the diverse nature of their personalities. Similarly, their capacity to look critically at their addiction is evident in their accounts of their struggle to overcome it. In other words, a complex and varied set of perspectives and experiences lies behind the common stereotypes that we have of drug addicts. It is partly this human dimension of the experience of drug addiction and the attempt to recover from it that we hope to convey in the book.

Previous work on recovery

Recovery from drug addiction is unquestionably a complex and multifaceted phenomenon. Many addicts recover on the basis of lengthy and extensive contact with drug-treatment agencies while others appear to recover without any recourse to treatment (Klingemann 1994). Indeed, it has been suggested that the proportion of addicts who manage to overcome their addiction without formal treatment may either match or be greater than the proportion who recover following treatment for their addiction (Waldorf and Biernacki 1979, Stall and Biernacki 1986, Cunningham 1999).

Over the years, numerous researchers from various disciplines have sought to understand the nature and dynamics of the process of recovery. One of the earliest and most widely quoted descriptions of the recovery from dependent drug use was Winick's claim in 1962 that addiction was, for the majority of addicts, a self-limiting process (Winick 1962). Basing his analysis on the arrest records of heroin addicts, which showed a diminishing number being arrested for drug-related offences with increasing age, Winick concluded that up to two-thirds of addicts 'mature out' of their addiction naturally by the time they reach their mid-thirties. Although the maturing-out thesis has been widely quoted in the addiction literature, in fact Winick provided very little information on how the process of maturation might operate apart from speculating that, as the addict matures with the passage of time, either the problems which led to the original drug use become less salient or the addict acquires alternative ways of dealing with them. While subsequent studies have confirmed that a high proportion of addicts do indeed appear to stop using drugs in their thirties (Waldorf 1983, Biernacki 1986, Prins 1994), the maturation thesis is increasingly seen as being only one of several explanations of how individuals may overcome their addiction (Prins 1994, Waldorf and Biernacki 1981). For example, Waldorf (1983) has identified five routes out of addiction in addition to maturing out: individuals can 'drift' out of addiction, become alcoholic or mentally ill, give up due to religious or political conversion, 'retire' by giving up the drug while retaining some aspects of the lifestyle, or change because their situation or environment has changed. The role of the latter, that is situational change, was demonstrated in a particularly striking way by Lee Robbins and various colleagues in their work on drug-taking among American servicemen. They noted, among other things, that many American servicemen who had developed extensive patterns of illegal drug use during the Vietnam War appeared to be able to cease or bring about a major reduction in their illegal drug use on returning to the United States. This, the authors believed, was largely a result of the servicemen's relocation to a range of social contexts in which drug-taking was neither encouraged nor facilitated (Robbins 1993). This work has been particularly influential in underlining the important role that social context may play, both in the development of drug misuse and in its reduction or elimination.

Some authors have sought to depict the recovery process in terms of a series of stages or phases. Frykholm (1985) describes three phases of addiction – experimental, adaptational and compulsive – in which the individual becomes an addict and three phases of de-addiction in which the process is reversed. De-addiction begins with a period of ambivalence in which the negative effects of drug use are increasingly felt and result in a gradual desire on the part of the addict to stop using drugs. This desire is offset in most cases by a continuation of the pleasurable effects of drug use and by the user's physical dependence on the drug. In the treatment phase, the addict's attempts at detoxification become more sustained and his or her drug-free periods grow longer. The addict perceives a need for 'external control and support' and so seeks help. According to Frykholm, in this phase the addict undergoes a 'radical reorientation' in which he or she suddenly experiences a desire to see him or herself in the role of ex-addict. The final stage of the model Frykholm calls emancipatory. This describes the period following detoxification when the addict is effectively an ex-addict and can remain off drugs without external assistance. One of the features of Frykholm's model is that it does not make provision for spontaneous recovery from addiction. By contrast, Waldorf's (1983) six-stage model of addiction does. His model describes three phases of becoming addicted – experimentation, escalation and maintaining – and a corresponding three stages of de-addiction. In the first stage of de-addiction, the dysfunctional or 'going through changes' phase, the negative effects of drug use begin to be felt and the addict may make forced or voluntary attempts to stop. These usually end in relapse. In the recovery phase the user makes a 'sincere' effort to give up drugs and may move away from the drug-using scene. The final phase he calls 'ex-addict'. According to Waldorf, recovery can occur with or without the help of treatment.

The most widely quoted model of the recovery process is associated with the work of Prochaska *et al.* (1992) who developed a five-stage model of recovery in which the individual progresses from a stage of 'precontemplation', before the user has considered stopping, to 'contemplation', when she or he begins to think about stopping, to 'preparation', in which the decision to stop occurs and efforts are made to prepare for stopping, to 'action' in which specific steps are taken to reduce drug use, and, finally, to 'maintenance', in which non-using behaviour is consolidated and the individual is now defined as an ex-addict.

While there is disagreement among authors as to the precise number and nature of the stages through which individuals may pass in overcoming their addiction, one feature which is common to many of the accounts in this area is the importance of a specific and identifiable 'turning point', a point at which the decision to give up drugs is taken and/or consolidated (Prins 1994, Simpson *et al.* 1986, Shaffer and Jones 1989). This decisive moment is variously described as an 'existential crisis' (Coleman quoted in Waldorf 1983), an 'epistemological shift' (Shaffer and Jones 1989) or, most commonly, as hitting 'rock bottom' (e.g. Maddux and Desmond 1980). Whatever the terminology used, the claim is that the addict has reached a point in his or her drug-using career beyond which she or he is not prepared to go. For some authors, this kind of crisis or turning point is an essential step on the road to recovery from addiction (Bess *et al.* 1972, Brill 1972). Moreover, according to the literature, this turning point is usually accompanied by some experience or event, which serves to stimulate or trigger the decision. These triggers are variable in nature and include things like a sudden deterioration in health, an adverse drug effect, being faced with the prospect of going to prison or the possible or actual loss of something important to the addict such as their partner, children or job (Stimson and Oppenheimer 1982, Waldorf and Biernacki 1981, Stall and Biernacki 1986).

Other researchers have sought to identify and describe the factors and circumstances which promote or impede the process of de-addiction. More specifically, a number of explanations have been proposed for the crucial decision to give up drugs. As Smart (1994) notes in his review of the literature on recovery from addiction, addicts themselves tend to give a variety of explanations for their decision to stop. In addition, the reasons which they give can vary substantially from study to study depending upon the design of the research. It is possible, however, to identify some of the more common and prominent themes in this work. A frequent explanation given in the literature is that addicts often simply burn out (Waldorf 1983, Biernacki 1986). Supporting a habit can be an exceptionally difficult and demanding routine and many addicts appear to become tired of dealing with the multiplicity of problems associated with maintaining their addiction. For example, Simpson *et al.* (1986) found that the main reason for addicts ceasing to use opiates was that they had had enough of the 'hustle' and were 'tired of the life'. Similarly, Frykholm (1985) found that the principal reason given for stopping was that the user was 'tired of the life of a street addict'. The 'burn out' explanation clearly has a close correspondence with the 'maturing out' thesis since both are the products of changes which could be said to occur naturally with the passage of time. A number of studies have also shown the influence of partners or children to be important in the decision to quit (Waldorf 1983, Frykholm 1985, Simpson *et al.* 1986, Smart 1994). In Waldorf's study of 201 ex-addicts, one-third of the sample said that pressure from significant others had played an import-ant part in their decision to give up drugs. This influence took the form of pressure and encouragement to stop, growing commitments to a family or partner and the fear of hurting or losing them. In their review of research on spontaneous recovery from addiction to alcohol, tobacco, food and illicit drugs, Stall and Biernacki (1986) found that family and friends were of primary importance both in initiating the recovery process and in sustaining it. Simpson *et al.* (1986) report that more than half (54 per cent) of their sample stated that 'family responsibilities' were an important element in their decision to quit while about a third (29 per cent) cited pressure from family members. It appears that the development of a new relationship can also be a significant factor in the decision to stop (Waldorf 1983, Simpson *et al.* 1986). A number of studies have also indicated that deteriorating health or fear of the emergence of health problems can provide the incentive to stop (Waldorf 1983, Vaillant 1983, Simpson *et al.* 1986). Other researchers have drawn attention to the occurrence of negative events in providing the motivation to change (Shaffer 1992, Edwards *et al.* 1992). For example, Waldorf (1983) reports that two out of five of his sample of ex-addicts reported a 'humiliating' experience, such as a spell in prison or ridicule by a friend, before deciding to give up while one-third referred to overdoses and deaths among drug-using friends or acquaintances as having been significant in their decision to stop.

However, while we know a good deal about the factors which correlate with exit from drug misuse (Smart 1994), we know relatively little about the cognitive processes through which the decision to stop using drugs occurs. In particular, the perceptual changes that are involved in this process are relatively unexplored. For example, what role, if any, do addicts' perceptions of themselves and their expectations of the future play in the decision to stop? An exception here is the work of Biernacki and Waldorf (Biernacki 1986, Waldorf 1983, Waldorf and Biernacki 1981). What is distinctive about the work of these researchers is that they have sought to explain the process of recovery from addiction in terms of the management of a spoiled identity. According to Biernacki (1986), the decision to stop taking drugs comes about when the user's addict identity conflicts with, and creates problems for, other identities that are unrelated to drug use – such as those of partner, parent or employee – in ways that are ultimately unacceptable to the user. For Biernacki (1986), the key to the recovery process lies in the realisation by addicts that their damaged sense of self has to be restored, combined with a re-awakening of their old identities and/or the establishment of new ones.

The research

The research on which this book is based is very much in the tradition of the work of Biernacki and his colleagues, with its emphasis on the role played by the individual's sense of identity in the process of recovery from dependent drug use. We also wanted to look at the process of recovery from the perspective of the addicts themselves and it is for this reason that we adopted a qualitative approach in the research by using semi-structured interviews as our method of data collection. From some perspectives, the number of people we have interviewed (70) may seem rather small. Other social science research has looked at samples of drug users in their hundreds or even thousands. However, we decided to study 70 recovering addicts rather than 700 because we wanted to explore the details rather than the generalities of their recovery. Our interest was not so much in counting responses but in understanding, in as much depth as possible, the process of recovery from the perspective of the recovering addicts themselves. In attempting to do this, we collected detailed information from each individual on how he or she faced up to and overcame addiction to illegal drugs.

The individuals in the study were interviewed after their recovery had taken place. We are aware of the potential difficulties associated with retrospective data of this sort; for example, the problem of recall and the possibility that events and circumstances might be reinterpreted or presented in ways that suit the individual's current presentation of self. The alternative would have been to have followed a cohort of addicts prospectively, interviewing them at regular intervals until such time as they recovered from their addiction. However, we rejected this possibility for the following reasons. First, while identifying a sample of addicts might have been relatively straightforward, the chaotic nature of their lives would have made tracking and re-interviewing them extremely difficult. Second, and perhaps more importantly, such a study would have had to be of a very long duration since addicts can remain on drugs for many years and there is no way of anticipating or predicting when they are likely to come off. All of this would have made a prospective study prohibitively expensive.

The sample of people interviewed in our research consisted of individuals who had, according to their own accounts, given up the drugs to which they had been addicted for a period of at least six months. It is important to stress at this point that it was not part of our research to try to check the accuracy of our interviewees' accounts of their recovery. There are a number of ways in which one might have sought to carry out such checks: for example, by requesting individuals to provide regular urine samples or by undertaking collateral interviews with nominated friends or partners. Neither of these options seemed to us to be particularly attractive as far as the present research was concerned. To have undertaken urine testing would have been to imply to the individuals we were interviewing that we did not fully trust their accounts of their recovery. It is difficult to see how that implication would not have had an impact on the relationships we were trying to establish with the individuals in the interview setting. Drug addicts are well used to interacting with people who assume that they cannot be trusted and are generally pretty worthless. To have asked our interviewees to provide us with a urine sample would have reinforced those perceptions. In addition, a urine sample is not a foolproof method of establishing whether or not a person is taking drugs. Different drugs are cleared from the body at different rates; heroin for example is cleared from the body within a matter of days whereas cannabis remains detectable within urine for upwards of two to three weeks. In order to prove the drug-using status of our interviewees, we would have had to have undertaken not a single urine test but multiple tests over many weeks or, possibly, months. Similarly, while we could have asked our interviewees to identify an individual within their social circle who could comment on their claim that they had stopped using drugs, we would have had no way of knowing whether or not these individuals were in a position to know. In a word, these collateral accounts would have been subject to similar doubts in their own right.

There will, of course, be those who will respond to what we have just said by asserting that it is impossible to accept what a recovering addict tells you at face value and it is simply naïve to do so. We believe that this is an overly cynical view and that it is likely to be inaccurate for the following reason. Quite simply, there was nothing for our interviewees to gain by misleading us about their drug use; we were neither paying them for the information they were providing nor were we rewarding their non-drug-using status in some other way. In fact, our respondents were giving up their time freely to participate in the study. In addition, we made it clear to them that we were interested in eliciting their own accounts of their drug use and recovery and that we wanted them to feel that they could tell us about their failures as well as their successes.

Some of the people we interviewed had, by their own admission, continued to use illegal drugs during the period when they considered themselves to have beaten their addiction. Most commonly, this drug use took the form of the occasional or, sometimes, the repeated use of cannabis, although other drugs might be used occasionally as well. However, for an individual to have moved from injecting heroin daily to even the daily use of cannabis would be regarded by most people as being a success and, certainly, that is the way in which the recovering addicts in our sample regarded those sorts of changes in their behaviour.

In total, interviews were carried out with 70 recovering addicts. These individuals were recruited from across Scotland by a variety of means: snowball sampling (25), follow-up of clients of drug services (17), and newspaper advertisement (28). The average age of our interviewees was 29.5 (range 20.2–45.3), the average length of drug use was 9.3 years (range 2–20 years), and 52 per cent of the sample was female. Most of our recovering addicts (60 out of 70) had received formal treatment of some kind for their addiction. While the great majority of our sample had been dependent upon opiates, most of the individuals interviewed in our research would be regarded as poly drug abusers in the sense that, at the height of their drug use, they were using a variety of illegal drugs. The average length of time for which our interviewees had ceased using their drug of choice was 4.3 years (range 7 months to 12 years). The interviews followed a loosely structured format in which individuals were encouraged to describe both the development of their drug use and their experience of coming off. Each interview lasted between 30 minutes and two hours, was audiotaped and entered into the Win-Max Pro software package for the analysis of textual data.

In analysing the interview material we adopted a grounded theory approach in order to allow the conceptual framework to emerge from the data (Glaser and Strauss 1967). In the first stage of the analysis, the data were reviewed in order to define concepts and identify patterns and relationships. In the second stage, these theoretical propositions were, in turn, subjected to systematic testing by means of the method of analytic induction (Denzin 1989). This involved reformulating the explanatory framework until we had been able to produce an explanation of the individuals' behaviour that accommodated the full range of things that were being said on a particular theme.

In researching and writing about the recovery from dependent drug use one inevitably confronts the problem of what term to use to describe someone who is recovering from an addiction to illegal drugs. Do you call them an ex-addict, a recovered addict or a recovering addict? Our preferred term in the book is 'recovering addict' not because it is the term which our interviewees used to refer to themselves – although some individuals did use this term – but because it portrays recovery as a process instead of as a fixed state.

2 Becoming and being addicted

Although the primary focus of this book is the process by which some addicts are able to come off illegal drugs, it is also important to appreciate the conditions and circumstances under which they became addicted in the first place. This is essential to an understanding of the place of drugs in these individuals' lives and of some of the significant issues they had to address in giving them up. Accordingly, in this chapter we begin by examining how and why the members of our sample first came to use illegal drugs. We then go on to explore the process by which they became addicts and to describe their experiences of living with and sustaining their addiction.

The first steps

The age at which our interviewees started to use drugs varied considerably as did the type of drug used. A typical pattern was one of experimentation with softer drugs in their early teens followed by progression to more powerful drugs and to regular use in their later teens or early twenties. According to the majority of our sample, their first introduction to mood-altering substances was with legally available products, most commonly solvents and alcohol. This usually took place between the ages of 12 and 14 years. Robin's account of his first experience with drugs was typical.

> My first experiences with drugs would be alcohol when I was about twelve, thirteen. Drinkin' half bottles o' wine an' bottles o' wine when you were twelve an' thirteen wasn't a big deal.
>
> *(Robin)*

For others, early experimentation might involve the use of magic mushrooms or various prescription drugs. For example, Fiona's drug use began with her taking her mother's Valium as a way of coping with a variety of stresses in her life.

> My Mam had the Valium. I was fourteen and I was under a lot of stress at school and my parents were getting separated so I thought, 'I'll try these'.
>
> *(Fiona)*

For most of our interviewees, their early experimentation with legal substances led eventually to the use of illegal drugs of which cannabis was initially the most popular. Around two-thirds of our interviewees reported having sampled illegal drugs by the time they were 15. This proportion is somewhat higher than that reported in surveys of young people, suggesting that the members of our sample were especially precocious as far as their initial drug-taking was concerned. For example, in a survey of over 7700 15- to 16-year-old school pupils in the UK, Miller and Plant (1996) reported that 42.3 per cent had tried an illegal drug while Parker and Measham (1994) found that 47 per cent of the same age group surveyed in the North West of England had done so. Although an even higher proportion (57 per cent) of 15- to 16-year-olds in Dundee, Scotland, were found by Barnard *et al.* (1996) to have tried illegal drugs, even that proportion falls considerably short of the figure for our sample.

In summary, the typical pattern of initiation into drug use described by our interviewees had two main characteristics: (1) an introduction to legal drugs in their early teens, and (2) a progression from legal to illegal substances. However, this pattern was not true of everyone. First, not all of our interviewees started taking drugs in their early teens. A small number (10) reported that their drug use started in their late teens or early twenties. Secondly, about a quarter of our sample reported that their first experience of drugs had been with illegal substances. Most commonly, this involved the use of 'softer' drugs such as cannabis, ecstasy, speed or LSD. However, for a small minority (4) their first experience was with 'hard' drugs. The latter were all women who started on heroin, three of them being introduced to the drug by partners who were either using or dealing in it.

Reasons for initial use of illegal drugs

Starting to take illegal drugs requires both motivation and opportunity and, as we will see, these two requirements are closely connected. According to our interviewees' accounts, the main reasons for their initial drug use were curiosity and a desire to comply with the expectations of others, especially those of their peer group. Of the two, curiosity was the explanation that was offered most often. Curiosity could be stimulated either by other people's accounts of their drug-taking or by observing directly the effects that drugs or other substances had upon them. More specifically, though, the root of our interviewees' curiosity was the fact that drug-taking was clearly enjoyable for those who took them. Quite simply, our sample were curious to know what it was about drugs that was so enjoyable and to experience that enjoyment for themselves.

> All ma pals at that time were doin' it round about me and the curiosity gets the better of you. I believe that's how most people get involved in drugs. They can blame it on this or blame it on that or whatever but at the end of the day most of us get involved in drugs 'cos our pals were doin' it and the curiosity gets the better of us.
>
> *(Joe)*

According to our interviewees, their initial experience of illegal drugs was, in most cases, a positive one. This, not surprisingly, had the effect of ratifying and reinforcing their decision to experiment with them. It was certainly an experience that nearly all of them wanted to repeat.

> Acid, I thought it was wild, because I had no inkling what drugs were, I'd heard of them but I didn't really understand what they were therefore I had no fear. I took this thing wondering what could happen . . . it was so small, one tablet, that in my head I couldn't fathom that it would do anything. It was like taking an aspirin, it wouldn't have any effect. Then it did, you know, and it was like 'wow' I've never felt anything like that in my life. And I guess it was so mind-blowing for me that first time and I enjoyed it.
>
> *(Nick)*

> My pal one night, we were in the house, this is the first time I ever took drugs. Her sister used to take drugs and she said to me one

night, try that. I tried it and it was some feelin' . . . it was great . . . It was a peaceful feelin' kind of . . . how can I explain the feelin' to somebody that's never took it? It wasn't like being drunk and being out of control . . . I wasn't fallin' about. It was just a feelin' of peace and contentment. It was a feelin' I liked . . . That was heroin, the very first time I took it.

(Maggie)

There was this stuff called LSD–100. I took them and I must have been about three days on this trip and the thought that went through ma mind was this is how I want to live.

(Glen)

The other main reason our interviewees gave for their initial experimentation with drugs was a desire to conform with, and be accepted by, their friends or, less commonly, their partners.

You ask ninety-nine per cent o' people, 'how did you get involved?' Ma mates were doin' it, ma girlfriend was doin' it or ma boyfriend was doin' it and you just get involved through that way.

(Stewart)

Of particular importance here was the individual's peer group, with the majority of our interviewees claiming that it had a major influence on their initial drug-taking. As the following extracts illustrate, the main motivating factor here appeared to be a desire for acceptance and a sense of belonging.

The reason was quite simple. My friends were all into takin' it. That was it, peer pressure I would say. All my friends were takin' it . . . it was like a social thing. If you weren't into it, you weren't in the in-crowd sort of thing.

(Douglas)

I started on cannabis when I was about fourteen and I think the reason I started doin' that was because all ma pals were doin' it. So I tried it and I liked the feelin' that I got.

(Maria)

However, our interviewees' accounts of the role of their peers in their introduction to drugs made little reference to what could be described as direct pressure from the group to engage in drug-taking. Bridie's experience of this sort of pressure was an exception.

> I always remember this lassie showin' me a tablet. And I refused it. And I was treated as a sort of outcast. Chicken, scaredy-cat, y'know. What's the problem that you're not wanting to take it?
>
> *(Bridie)*

More commonly, compliance with the group appeared to be of a more voluntary and self-imposed nature. Individuals simply joined in the activity because their friends were doing it and not because their friends forced them to participate. This conclusion is consistent with the work of a number of researchers who have recently challenged the hitherto conventional wisdom that one of the main influences on initial drug use is peer pressure (Coggans and McKellar 1994, Bauman and Ennett 1996, Reed and Rowntree 1997, Hart and Hunt 1997, Lloyd 1998). These authors, and others, have argued that peer selection – the process by which young people choose to associate with like-minded individuals – and individual choice are more important than peer pressure in the process of initiation into drug use. While we have no data on the extent to which the individuals in our study selected their friends on the basis of their inclination to use drugs, the importance of individual choice is borne out by the part which curiosity apparently played in the decision to experiment with various substances.

Among our sample, initial drug use nearly always took place in the company of others. This corresponds closely with the findings of other studies (Parker *et al.* 1998, Mayock 2000). As we have already indicated, the most usual context was the individual's peer group but occasionally a partner or relative would be present. In addition to providing a large part of the motivation for trying drugs, these significant others fulfilled two other very important functions as far as the individual's introduction to drugs was concerned. Firstly, they were instrumental in making the drug available and, therefore, in providing the opportunity to try it. In the absence of its supply by peers, it is unlikely that individuals would have set out to obtain the drug on their own. Eddie's introduction to cannabis was fairly typical.

> I started off smokin' hash. Just me and my mates, we were campin' at the back of my house one day and one of my mates

came up and said, 'I've got a bit o' dope, d'you fancy havin' a smoke?' I didn't know what it was at that time. I was about fourteen or fifteen at the time. And I says, 'Aye, come on we'll go in the tent and have a smoke.' So we started smokin' and it just sort of progressed from there.

(Eddie)

Secondly, the peer group provided a supportive environment in which the individual could experiment with and learn about drugs. Since the effects of consuming certain drugs are not always immediately positive, part of this role involved supporting the novice through negative experiences and encouraging him or her to persevere. In the following extract, Bill describes how he was persuaded by his friends to try temgesics again after a bad initial experience with the drug.

I would say temgesics I got into first. Basically I just tried them because the boys I was goin' about with were takin' them and I thought I'll give it a crack just like anythin' else you know. So I took them and basically they just made me sick. That's what I can't understand . . . they made me very, very sick and I still went back to it. I took them again because I was told the next time you'll not be sick, you build an immunity.

(Bill)

However, it is not simply a matter of perseverance. As Howard Becker (1963) described in his classic account of marijuana use, *Outsiders*, novices frequently need to be instructed by experienced users in how to take a drug and in how to interpret the experience of using it. In the following passage, one of our interviewees recounts his own learning experience and describes the process of learning to smoke cannabis successfully as being akin to serving an apprenticeship.

The hash thing was always around. I always thought people that smoked that stuff were a bit nutty, simply because it didn't affect me. That was because I wasn't smokin' it right. It wasn't until this mate of mine actually showed me how. I think it's true of any drug you use. Certainly later on when you go on to snort and inject and things, you have to be shown how to do it. If you had been smoking a joint, I had to be shown how to take blasts or tokes or whatever and to hold that in and just maybe even seal it with your last blast. And then I understood what being stoned on hash was. In fact I was sick the first time. I always found when I was taking drugs a lot of the time I wasn't really enjoying it but pretending I was enjoying it. Simply because I was in amongst these people. It was like, 'great that eh Nick?' And I'd go, 'Aye'. And it wasn't great, I was really feelin' quite lousy, but I used to pretend . . . These days it's different but I feel I actually did an apprenticeship. That may sound crazy but I feel that I served my apprenticeship taking drugs.

(Nick)

While curiosity and a desire to conform were offered as the main reasons for our interviewees' initial experimentation with drugs, a minority indicated that a belief that it would have a positive effect upon their image and status was also important. For instance, Brenda believed that her drug-taking had a certain status and glamour attached to it through its association with pop stars and other prominent figures.

Curiosity always got the better of me . . . you know the bits and pieces that you hear and read in the papers . . . It was an image thing y'know, there was a big sort of thing attached to it, y'know. The pop stars did it, the pop stars died of it, it was acceptable, you were almost sort of, in a certain way you were looked up to in a way.

(Brenda)

In the following extract, Tom describes how he associated smoking cannabis with images of adulthood and male toughness.

I got introduced to dope, hash, by some older friends and we were smokin' it in one of their houses when their parents were out. I remember feelin' quite sick but at the same time pretty stoned. I felt like a hard man and I was a grown-up now 'cos I was smokin' dope. I thought it was a big thing to do.

(Tom)

According to our interviewees' accounts, their experimentation with illegal drugs was seldom initiated as a way of attempting to cope with problems in their lives. Indeed, some of them were quite adamant that this was not the case.

Everything was fine. I'd just had a new baby. I was quite happy. You know I don't always believe that . . . the psychiatrist used to come out with that all the time, 'Well there must have been a problem for me to take heroin in the first place?' But it's not true, that's not true.

(Kate)

However, for a small minority of our sample the ability of the drug they were using to numb the mind and ease psychological pain was, it would appear, their primary reason for deciding to use it. For example, Linda and Bernadette were clear that their initial drug use was prompted by a desire to 'escape' from some internal or external reality which they found difficult to live with.

I needed somethin', I was looking for somethin' out there to make me feel better than what I was feeling. I always thought to myself if it takes away how I inwardly feel about myself then that's what I'm lookin' for.

(Linda)

At that stage, if you're taking drugs, you're taking drugs to hide from things you can't cope with. Especially if a situation comes, you just use that as the answer . . . it was just stuff to get you out of your face, rather than just think about anything. And that's just the way you deal with things . . . you're takin' it to sort of escape from things.

(Bernadette)

Clearly, then, a number of factors appeared to be involved in promoting the initial use of illegal drugs. Most of our sample began because it was enjoyable and daring and enabled them to comply with the norms of their social group. To that extent, then, it was largely a product of young people's desire to experiment and of their need for companionship and a sense of belonging. The peer group played a central part in the process of initiation since it was usually in the context of this body that the individual's curiosity was both stimulated and satisfied. Not only did the peer group make the drugs available, it also engendered interest in them by exposing the individual to their use and, in particular, their effect upon others.

However, whichever route they took into illegal drugs, without exception our interviewees reported that, when they began to use them, they were completely confident that they would not become addicted. Addiction was something that happened to other people; our interviewees believed, at the time, that they would be able to use the drug on their own terms and to resist its power. Maggie and Harry were typical.

> She said try some smack and we snorted it for the first time, liked it and then she used to get wee bits and give me it. She used to say to me, 'you can get a habit', 'cos her sister had a habit. But I said, 'No, it'll never happen to me, I know what I'm doin'.' Thinking I had it right under control. But I didn't.
>
> *(Maggie)*

> It was just like a phase we were going through, we just wanted to experiment. We thought at the time taking cannabis seemed fairly harmless, so we thought, well let's try other drugs and see what like they are. And we obviously read that heroin was really addictive and everything like that, but when we tried it we thought there was no way we were going to get addicted. And we really, really believed that. We were so strong willed y'know. It was like we're only just trying this one time to see what it's like, y'know. And it ended up we all got hooked.
>
> *(Harry)*

As we will see, our interviewees' confidence in their ability to avoid becoming dependent was badly misplaced. All went on to become regular users and addicts.

Becoming a regular user

While the majority of experimental and occasional drug users do not go on to become addicted, the members of our sample, by definition, did. Following their initial introduction to illegal drugs and their use on an occasional basis, the next stage was progression to regular use. Our interviewees offered a number of explanations for this transition. Some claimed that they started to use drugs regularly for the simple reason that they enjoyed their use and could see no good reason to stop. Even when using illegal drugs regularly, they remained confident that they would not become addicted and the pleasure derived from their drug-taking was, according to them, immense.

> I just liked gettin' out of my face back then basically. That's it, I loved gettin' out of my face. I loved the feelin' from smack.
>
> *(Mary)*

> I thought that when I found heroin it was the answer to all ma problems and this was it. I'd found what I'd been lookin' for. 'Cos the feelings I was getting from it at first . . . I mean was amazin'.
>
> *(Dorothy)*

Most commonly, however, progression to regular use appeared to be the outcome of a process of unconscious 'drift' rather than the result of a deliberate decision to use more often. What usually happened was that the user's habit grew insidiously, and almost imperceptibly, with the individuals gradually taking larger quantities of the drug or increasing the frequency with which they took it until it became a regular part of their lives. Judy and Dion describe in the following extracts how they made the transition to regular use without any real sense of volition.

> It progressed. I did it at the weekend then it became the weekends and Wednesday night and then it became a Thursday night until it started controllin' me. Then I needed it, so it became I did it every night.
>
> *(Judy)*

> I started takin' methadone for no apparent reason really. I was just offered it. I was offered it at a party at a friend's house. To be honest I was feeling a bit down and I shouldn't have done anything as silly as that. However I took it and within an hour and a half I felt, well it was far better than any alcohol, a relaxing experience. And I was on night duty at the time as well, sort of part-time work, and I started to take it during night duty as well. But, of course, the tolerance soon went up then sooner or later you get into a bit of a fix really. At first you used to take it as a treat, even be able to control it, say take it on certain days, Fridays and Saturdays and things. But then eventually you began to take it every night, or every other night. I stopped working,

I couldn't keep up with work, I was on income support and all my money went on drugs really. It took a long time before I went to the doctor and asked him for a prescription. But from first starting on methadone to being addicted to it took about six weeks, not long at all.

(Dion)

Often, progression to regular use of illegal drugs was heavily influenced by the individuals' relationships with their partners or their membership of their peer group since these relationships provided both the opportunity and the encouragement to use more regularly. Those who were introduced to drugs by a partner who was a regular user rapidly became regular users themselves. Similarly, membership of a group in which drug-taking was common practice encouraged the development of a regular habit. As Kevin reported, 'it was just that everybody followed each other like sheep. Everybody did it.' In short, individuals fell into line with the rest of the group.

According to some of our interviewees, boredom resulting from unemployment or poor recreational facilities served to heighten the appeal of regular drug use by helping to fill a void in their lives.

Q   So what was going on in your life when you started using hash heavier and began looking for heavier stuff? What was going on then?

R   Nothin', just boredom. Nothin' to do, nothin', no place to go at night or anythin'. So it was just somethin' to do to relieve the boredom.

(Phil)

While only a small minority of our sample reported starting to take drugs as a way of coping with problematic aspects of their lives, once they had encountered the pleasurable or 'therapeutic' effects of their drug-taking, this often became an important reason for continuing or for more regular use. For some of our interviewees, regular drug-taking helped them to cope with psychological or social traumas which they found difficult to deal with in other ways; for example, a violent home, a history of sexual abuse or, in Wendy's case, the loss of a child.

R   Once I started takin' I thought to myself, this is pretty good, it sort of blocks a lot of things out.

Q   What were you trying to block out?

R   I think it was losin' the bairn [child], it seemed to be just a
     wee bit easier to handle, y'know. Obviously it was still
     there, but it didn't feel as hard.

(Wendy)

Many of our interviewees referred to their use of drugs as an 'escape'
from reality or as a way of numbing psychological pain and helping them
to feel better. As Rhona put it, 'If you've got a lot of problems and you
start taking drugs you don't worry about the problems. In fact, you don't
think you've got any problems.' In other words, a crucial step for many
on the road to regular drug use was the association of drug-taking with
feeling better about oneself and one's life. This finding corresponds with
the consensus in the literature that the risk of drug addiction is closely
associated with the experience of serious problems and adversities (see
Hawkins *et al.* 1992, Lloyd 1998).

For other members of our sample, regular drug use was employed to
help overcome feelings of personal inadequacy. Drug-taking was said to
be a particularly effective antidote to shyness or lack of confidence.

I was over-anxious, over-sensitive, very inhibited, insecure, lacked
confidence, self-esteem, these characteristics were there, that's
why I feel there's no doubt the first time I injected, the first time
I came into contact, it was just like we were made for each other.

(Colin)

When you take any kind of drugs it does you a wee favour. It
takes away your worries, it takes away your inhibitions, it takes
away your self-doubt . . . takes it all away. It does you a right
favour. It helps you out.

(Jimmy)

It could also counteract feelings of loneliness or isolation.

I was on my own and I had nobody else around me. It was just
like me and the kids. I got really, really lonely and I hated bein'
lonely. I got scared when I was lonely. And when I used drugs I
was never lonely.

(Maria)

Helen described her heroin habit as being like having a 'lover'.

> You don't really get lonely on smack. It's like having a lover and that's what it's like. If you've got your habit, well for me anyway, I wasn't lonely.
>
> *(Helen)*

For the majority of our sample, regular drug use was not explained in terms of a single cause. Most of their accounts suggest that usually a combination of factors was involved and that frequently the kinds of things that we have just described acted in concert. For example, Suzie talked about how drugs served both to block out certain memories and to boost her confidence and self-esteem.

> I couldn't cope with life, with the problems in life. A lot had happened to me, I had experienced some tragics in ma life and the only way of dealin' with them was to get out of ma face. It was takin' the soreness away from me. I was hurtin' and it was taking the hurt away. Other times you would just get high because you thought you were cool when you were high, 'cos you had confidence that you don't really have in yourself . . . there's different reasons why you take it.
>
> *(Suzie)*

The progression to regular use is, then, explicable principally in terms of the pleasurable, mood-enhancing effects of the drugs being used and their attendant ability to deal with feelings of unhappiness. In short, for a time at least, drug-taking makes people feel good and, of course, because it makes people feel good, it is not surprising that it has a particular appeal to those who, for whatever reason, feel bad about themselves or their lives.

An escalating habit

Alongside their progression to regular use, another important change took place in our interviewees' drug habits. In every case their use of drugs escalated in the sense that they all began to use drugs with increased frequency and to use ever more powerful substances. In addition, many of them started to inject the drugs they were using. Our recovering addicts' accounts suggest that the process of escalation was driven by two related factors: first, a continuing desire to experiment and to find new 'highs' and, second, the need to satisfy ever-rising tolerance thresholds.

According to our interviewees, in the initial stages of their career as a regular user, the desire to experiment and to acquire new and different drug-induced experiences was high.

> And from then it just led, the usual progression into acid and stuff like that, back in the days when acid was acid. Other things like speed, amphetamines. At that age, twenty-one, you think you're goin' to live forever. 'Aye just give us that, stoned man, give us that.' Everythin's OK, know'.
>
> *(Frank)*

One consequence of this was that many of our addicts found themselves using a combination of drugs, often at the same time. In other words, multiple drug use was an extremely common feature of our users' habits.

> It was just like every drug, there wasn't one particular drug like, I was on everything, any drug and every drug.
>
> *(Malky)*

> And what started happenin' after I started usin' the needles was that with the heroin, I started mixin' drugs. Mixin' heroin with temazepam, and other sleeping tablets and stuff. Anythin' I was just takin' anythin' and everythin' I could get ma hands on. I went right through the card, there's nothin' I've not used and I don't say that 'cos it's somethin' to be proud of, but it's the way it was.
>
> *(Dorothy)*

As Claire explains, graduation to more powerful drugs also partly developed out of a desire for a more satisfying high.

> I was curious about that [heroin] because I'd tried everything else and obviously once you've tried somethin' you're not getting the same buzz out of it anymore. So I was wanting to go on and try other things. And there was a crowd who all used heroin at the

time – some of them were snortin' it, some of them were injectin' it. And I wanted to try a bit of that.

(Claire)

In part, the nature and pace of escalation were determined by those with whom the user associated. These significant others could be an individual, such as a partner, or more commonly a group of users. Different groups and individuals had different patterns of use and favoured different drugs. They also provided access to new drug-induced experiences and to different ways of taking drugs. This meant, for example, that users were considerably more likely to progress to heroin and/or to inject if those practices were pursued by their partner or by the group of users to which they belonged.

According to our interviewees, the other major factor behind their escalating drug use was the need to satisfy the ever-increasing demands of their addiction. One of the characteristic features of drug addiction is the fact that, as tolerance levels rise, increasing amounts of the drug have to be taken in order to achieve the desired effect. Satisfying this need could mean either moving on to more powerful substances or taking more of the same drug.

We were introduced to heroin. The temgesics weren't doin' anythin' for us anymore, they were just, it was a normal way of livin' . . . we couldn't feel normal without them, but we didn't get the buzz off them we used to.

(Bridie)

Basically I had a very, very high tolerance and your tolerance grows along with the habit so obviously what you first started takin' doesn't do you any good anymore. You need more, you need more quantity.

(Ian)

One of the most significant steps that a drug user can take is to start taking drugs intravenously. Its significance resides in the fact that it is an invasive procedure which both heightens the risk of overdose and introduces additional hazards such as the risk of contracting HIV, hepatitis C and other blood-borne infections. Many of our interviewees recognised the decision to inject as having been a significant step in their drug career. It was also one which most of them claimed to have been reluctant to take. However, the reason for their reported reluctance was not the risks and hazards associated with intravenous use. Instead their resistance appeared to be a product of apprehension regarding the actual process of injecting. In particular, most of our interviewees reported having had a deep-seated fear of 'needles'. In addition, of course, injecting oneself is not something that an individual automatically knows how to do. Consequently nearly all of those who progressed to intravenous drug use reported requiring, and receiving, help with learning how to do it. Usually their first intravenous 'hit' was administered by others and this would usually continue until they felt able to do it by themselves. For example, Stewart and Helen described how other users helped them to overcome their fear of syringes and to learn how to inject themselves.

> I remember being terrified of needles so one of your pals would give you it, but you had to learn how to give a hit.
>
> *(Stewart)*

> I had to hold my arm out and not look. I didn't know how to do it, and after a while it was like, hey you're going to have to learn to do this yourself. I know you don't want to but . . .
>
> *(Helen)*

As Debbie explained, often the main incentive to doing it oneself was the cost involved in getting others to do it since the latter usually required payment for their services in the form of drugs.

> I couldn't inject maself. I couldn't do it. For a couple of weeks I had to run about the streets and get people to do it for me and to get people to do it for me I had to give them a bit of ma drugs. So eventually I got sick of it one night. I think it was about one in the mornin' and I was out lookin' for somebody, know just for them to inject this drug into me . . . I couldn't do it myself, but eventually I went up to the house and that's when I did it myself. I was fed up. And I just remember puttin' the needle in my arm in the vein and drawin' blood and it was just a relief havin' that in my system. I just wanted that in my system as quickly as possible.
>
> *(Debbie)*

The individual's first experience of taking drugs intravenously could vary considerably. For most, such as Sharon and Bridie, it appears to have been an entirely positive experience.

It was one of the guys who I was scorin' off of. It was his brother, married with kids and that. I'd offered him a bit o' smack if he would give me the injection and he said 'aye'. So I went up to his house and he gave me ma first hit . . . Amazin'. There's nothin' else I can say about it . . . the effect of the drug and everythin', I was hooked straight away. I never went back to snortin' really or smokin' unless at that time I couldn't get hold of works.

(Sharon)

Injecting. He told me the effect would come on me quicker. With snortin' it took about twenty minutes to come on, but injectin' it goes into your bloodstream right away. So I was thirteen when I had ma first hit and . . . I always remember 'cos I stuck ma arm out and was going, 'Is it over is it over?' And I didn't feel nothin', and I remember . . . sayin' to myself 'this is great'. Know, I felt brilliant, just the effect it gave me. And I thought I'd cracked it, thought I'd found the thing that would make me feel the way I wanted to feel.

(Bridie)

For a minority, though, the experience was not a positive one. For instance, Eddie was disappointed that he did not experience the sort of high he had been expecting when he had his first 'hit' of heroin.

From what I was expecting I was disappointed, I was disappointed in the feeling I got because I didn't get the feeling that everybody was saying. You know this rush, I didn't get the rush.

(Eddie)

Graham reported that it made him feel extremely ill.

He got this guy to give me a hit intravenously; first intravenous drug use for me and it was the worst experience of my life . . . I was just ill, I was sick, y'know, constantly, all the time. Couldn't eat, couldn't drink, couldn't do anything. He took me up to his sister's house and we just kind of stayed there the night, I just lay on a floor all night, couldn't move or anything. And then I vowed, y'know, you leave heroin, y'know, never touch it again.

(Graham)

However, all of those who initially had negative experiences continued to persevere and eventually became intravenous drug users.

The difficulties associated with intravenous drug use raise the question of why individuals were attracted to it at all. In other words, what was its appeal? Some of our interviewees appear to have been attracted to it out of curiosity and a vague sense that they might be missing out on something.

> I was like, 'what's this all about?' I just used to sit around the house and . . . see other older guys in and out [of] the kitchen, blood y'know, I was curious to see what they were doin', what am I missing out on. So anyway I got offered some so that was really the first time I'd injected.
>
> *(Malky)*

> His big brother's mates, they were all into . . . usin' drugs as well. So when I was sittin' in the house they'd be comin' in and usin' needles and that. So when you see what's goin' on round you, you think well maybe I'll try that.
>
> *(Kevin)*

However, most of the addicts who went on to use drugs intravenously did so quite deliberately and for two very specific reasons. Firstly, it was cheaper and secondly, it produced a quicker and more pronounced effect.

> I really started injecting 'cos I wasn't gettin' the buzz that I was used to gettin', I wasn't gettin' the same buzz snortin' so I was buying more of the drug. You need more all the time. So I started injectin' it.
>
> *(Maggie)*

> All my old mates were injecting and I got my bit and I was going to snort it and somebody said, 'you know you're wasting it doing that'. And I thought 'what do you mean wasting it?' And they said 'you're not getting the full buzz, you're not getting the rush'. And it was like hmmm, and that's how they got me attracted. 'Cos I had to get a rush. You can't explain that to people now, but it's worth having, well it seemed to be worth having at the time and that was it, the needle.
>
> *(Nick)*

> I snorted it to begin with. I did that for a couple of months, snortin' it and then listenin' to other people tellin' me that you're better jaggin' it, you get the effects quicker and you don't need to use as much. So that's what I started doin'.
>
> *(Claire)*

Recognising addiction

The recognition by individuals that they were addicted could take anything from a few weeks to several months or even years depending upon the drug being used and the addicts' ability to support their habit. As we saw earlier, nearly all of the addicts in our sample believed initially that they would not become addicted and, indeed, many of them were able to continue using illegal drugs for some time before being forced to accept the reality of their dependence upon them. For the great majority of our sample, the recognition that they were addicted usually came with the experience of withdrawal symptoms and the realisation that they needed drugs simply to be able to function normally. They were no longer in control of their drug-taking; it was controlling them. The catalyst for this realisation varied for different individuals. For some, like Debbie, it was prompted by the realisation that they needed the drug to be able to start the day.

> I was waking up in the morning with stomach cramps, muscle pains and it's just a horrible feelin' when you wake up in the morning and you really need to get a bit of kit, know what I mean, just horrible. That's when you know you're dependent on it, you need it.
>
> *(Debbie)*

However, for the great majority of our sample, the realisation that they were addicted came when they were for some reason deprived of the means of supporting their habit. For Bernadette, this happened when her father confined her to the house and her access to drugs was cut off.

> Q   When did you first start to see your usage as a problem?
>
> R   The police went up to my mother's door and pointed out that I was hanging about with sort of the wrong crowd, and

they told my dad . . . to check my arms. Then my dad came out lookin' for me, found me, went up to the house, and I realised when I was kept in that I needed it. Then, I started havin' withdrawals.

(Bernadette)

For others such as Michael it was ending up in prison that separated them for the first time from the drugs they had been using and imposed the realisation that they had become dependent upon them. Until that point it had apparently never occurred to Michael that he might be addicted and, indeed, he even appears to have not, at first, made a connection between his withdrawal symptoms and his enforced abstinence.

I can remember the very first time I got the jail and I lay in the police station overnight 'cos I wasn't givin' them my right name. And they held me in overnight for trying to be smart. And that was the very first time I experienced withdrawal symptoms. 'Cos people are always telling you the good side to it, about what it's goin' to be like when you get this buzz and this stone and how amazing it's goin' to be. They never tell you what it's like when you really become involved. And I can [remember] that first night in the police station, and I was shoutin', 'you better get me a doctor, there's somethin' wrong with me'. And 'cos I was [vomiting] up all over the place and had sickness and diarrhoea and one minute I was sweating and the next minute I was freezing and my legs were all jittery and there was pains in ma stomach. I felt as if somebody had kicked fuck right out of me . . . that's how I felt . . . couldn't sleep or anythin' like that either. And the copper's [police officer] laughing at me. He knew what it was that was wrong with me and he's standing saying, 'did your pals not tell you about this?' As I said, that was the first time I ever experienced the withdrawal symptoms. But, as soon as I got out the next day, I went straight for a hit and that was me, within seconds I was brand-new again. So that was me, I wasn't usin' it for fun anymore, I was usin' it 'cos I had to use it.

(Michael)

However, the most common cause of being deprived of drugs was a lack of money and, for the majority of the addicts in our sample, it was when they found themselves unable to purchase drugs that their dependence was brought home to them.

> We weren't drug addicts we were just boys, cocky and arrogant. Then one day we couldn't get it and that was when we realised we were addicted to it.
>
> *(Douglas)*

For some of our interviewees, the realisation that they had become dependent appeared to come very quickly. Jane and Suzie both reported recognising that they had become addicted within the first few weeks of starting.

> Q So how did you start to develop a habit with it?
>
> R Very quickly, before you know it, it's got a hold of you. It can happen within a week. Maybe within a week to two weeks if you've not got it you're not well. So you're takin' another wee bit to take that not wellness away. And, before you know it you're getting worse and worse. In the end I was takin' it because I had to take it. I wasn't takin' it because I wanted to take it. I wasn't gettin' any enjoyment out of it.
>
> *(Jane)*

> Q When did you realise you were hooked on it?
>
> R Just a few weeks after it started. I couldn't believe it catches up on you so fast. I didn't like to admit to myself I was hooked on it, but I was gettin' up in the morning and I couldn't do anything without havin' it . . . looking back now I could say that that's how quickly it affected me. Within the two weeks, you know, getting up every mornin' and going to steal somethin' to get money, or stealing off ma dad for a bag just to get [through] the day.
>
> *(Suzie)*

For others the realisation took considerably longer, essentially because they had the financial means to ensure an uninterrupted supply of the drugs they were using. For example, Judy was protected from the reality of her addiction because her dealer partner kept her supplied regularly for three years.

> Yeah, for three years I carried on using not knowin' I could get addicted to it. Not knowin' I was addicted to it because I never

had a chance, not a day went by that I didn't have it . . . so I never felt any withdrawals 'cos he was dealing it. It was always there. I had it for three years every single day so I never had a chance to withdraw and understand that side of it.

(Judy)

In Joyce's case the moment of truth only arrived when her savings became exhausted.

Aye it was all right at first for about two years 'cos I had money, money in the bank . . . but once the money went down that's when I realised I had a problem. I didn't see the problem before 'cos I always had money and I was able to do things other people did so I thought I was all right, I didn't have a problem. I could just stop it. So I thought.

(Joyce)

It is clear from our interviewees' accounts that being deprived of the drugs they were using, for whatever reason, was absolutely fundamental to the realisation that they were addicted. In the absence of such enforced abstinence, and its physical consequences, it was possible to maintain the belief that, while they were using drugs, it was out of choice and they were not dependent on them. As Claire and Stewart pointed out, apart from the experiences associated with withdrawal, there was little to indicate when the user had become addicted.

There's no sign that says, 'you're now entering addiction', there's no big sign that says, 'you'll need to stop now, if you go once more that's you'. You just cross that line and you don't realise you've crossed it until you try to stop. I didn't think about withdrawal symptoms or anything like that 'cos I always had access to money.

(Stewart)

You don't know when you're becoming an addict . . . all the way through using there's no barrier you cross to tell you you are now entering addiction. You find this out when you're lying strung out and don't know what's wrong with you.

(Claire)

Only very seldom were other factors or events cited by our interviewees as prompting the realisation that they had become addicted. An exception was Judy who was informed that she was an addict after having been admitted to hospital with severe liver disease.

> I was on for three years before I realised I was addicted and, even then, when I got told I was a heroin addict, I didn't really understand it because nobody explained it to me . . . I ended up in hospital, my liver collapsed and I had hepatitis B and I was in hospital for six months and I was on a life support machine for three months of that, which I can't remember. All I can remember is collapsing up at my father's house and waking up three months later and gettin' told I'm a drug addict.
>
> *(Judy)*

Very occasionally, friends or, more commonly, family members would inform the addict that they thought he or she had a problem with drugs. However, according to the addicts' recollections, this appeared to occur less frequently than one might expect. This may have been partly because the addiction would often be kept hidden from the addict's family and partly, perhaps, because some addicts' families apparently chose either to deny that there was a problem or to simply ignore it.

> I was always in the toilet, I spent about a year in the toilet . . . And I had the cheek to flush the pan as if I was doin' the toilet know, I'd spend about half an hour pure mad with it hittin' up in the toilet know. Your family would be in saying, 'a bit of blood in that sink, where did that come from?' And I'd [say] ma finger was cut. I think your family . . . they don't want to see it. They know it's there but they don't want to say.
>
> *(Pauline)*

On those occasions in which family members did seek to raise the fact that the addict had a problem with drugs it would usually be dismissed or denied. As long as they could sustain their habit and avoid the distress of withdrawal, they could maintain the belief that they were in control.

In summary, then, by far the most significant factor in promoting the awareness that they were addicted was being deprived of the drugs they were using and experiencing the physical consequences of unsatisfied dependence. However, realising that one was addicted and perceiving that addiction as a problem could be very different things. Some of our interviewees reported having been quite content to continue with their habit even when they realised that they were dependent upon it. They continued to derive pleasure from their drug use and saw no reason to stop.

Q   Did you not think then it was a problem?

R   Well not really 'cos . . . I still liked doin' it. I loved usin' drugs. I loved it, it was great. Best feelings I've had in my life was with my drug-takin'.

(Kenny)

Heroin, I loved heroin 'cos that stopped ma head racing. That totally numbed me. Valium, temazepam calmed me down. But nothing like smack. Smack's excellent. This is me with ma junkie head on again.

(Angela)

Douglas was able to support his habit together with what he believed was an attractive lifestyle as a dealer. In fact, things were so good that he claimed it would have been 'silly' for him to have given up the life.

I just carried on. It sounds daft but when you haven't got anything that's when you want help, you've got no money or that. But see when you're doing alright you don't want help. I was always doin' OK. I started selling heroin so I didn't need any help. I had all the heroin I wanted. I was Mr Big if you like. I had money and cars and that. You thought you were 'it', you know, Jack the Lad. You were gettin' girls you know what I mean. Why stop . . . that's every boy's fantasy to have women, drugs, money, fast cars. So why would I want to go into a rehab you know, why would I? It was silly.

(Douglas)

Other interviewees found aspects of the drug-using lifestyle exciting.

Aye, I was just about eighteen round about this time. So that was me, I started injectin' it. I was out shoplifting every day by this time. 'Cos I was young and daft and caught up in that scene and I thought that was all great being in amongst all these shoplifters.

(Lisa)

As long as these addicts were able to sustain their habit it was not seen as a problem, especially if they were able to support it through legal means.

> I enjoyed it, and . . . at that point, it wasn't causing any hassle. I wasn't out stealin' or anythin' for it, I was out working. And I didn't honestly think it was a problem at all. I enjoyed it, it was exciting.
>
> *(Bernadette)*

> I was still goin' into work every day, y'know, all through. As long as I got my smack every day, as long as I could keep myself straight, I could function no problem. I never saw myself as a junkie. I didn't do the usual junkie things 'cos I'd started from the top of the pile sort of thing. I didn't start off with the usual sort of route, y'know, screwing [robbing] people's houses to get money for your next fix and all that sort of stuff.
>
> *(Frank)*

In addition, the effects of the drug itself could help to close the addicts' minds to the reality of their situation. As Kathleen put it when describing her experience with heroin, it imparts 'a feeling of security'.

> And that was the main thing with heroin, it gives you a feeling of security. I can say this in retrospect because at the time you don't realise this. There's just a whole feeling of security. You just shut the whole world out.
>
> *(Kathleen)*

For these addicts, then, their addiction only became a 'problem' when they were unable to support their habit or, as we shall see, when the activities required to sustain it became problematic.

Living with addiction

Irrespective of whether the addicts regarded their addiction as a problem or not, once they had become dependent their lives became dominated by the need to feed their habit and to secure the means of doing so. As the following extracts reveal, addiction was an extremely hard taskmaster. Its demands were all-consuming and our interviewees repeatedly referred to the comprehensive way in which the needs of their habit took over their lives.

> My whole life, my whole being was centred on drugs and any means to get them you know. My whole life revolved around drugs, drugs, drugs.
>
> *(Kenny)*

> You know nothin' else matters, nothin' matters except gettin' your next fix. That's your main object, your only object in life.
>
> *(Frank)*

Some of our sample described how self-centred their addiction had made them.

> When you're takin' drugs you don't give a fuck. Once you're involved with it, you only care about yourself. I remember times arguing with her [mother], 'it's ma life I'll do what I want with it, I'm not affecting anybody else if I want to ruin ma life' . . . It was only when I came off it I noticed the disruption I'd caused in ma family.
>
> *(Charlie)*

This self-centredness could even involve neglecting or disregarding one's own children.

> It was pretty heavy 'cos we had kids running about . . . two wee kids running around that really weren't being looked after. I couldn't have cared less at that point, d'you know what I mean?
>
> *(Nancy)*

> My oldest boy and my wee one started seeing me hittin' . . . I wasn't givin' a shit if the kids were seein' me when I hit or anythin' like that. Just get the hit over and done with. Never mind, if they wouldn't go out of the room. Bad attitude.
>
> *(Laura)*

Nearly all of our interviewees also described losing respect for their own appearance, personal hygiene or well-being.

I used to be a clean person, my hair, my appearance. When I took [drugs] that all went and I used to have the same clothes on for weeks on end . . . stinking, not caring . . . as I say, these things don't matter when you've got a drug habit. They just go out the window.

(Maggie)

Feeding the habit

The addicts' single, overriding preoccupation was to obtain money to purchase drugs. As we have seen, little else mattered. Moreover, the power of the drug was such that they would do anything to get it. At first, legitimate means might be employed; for instance, savings might be used or possessions might be sold.

The money was just totally unbelievable at this point. I sold all my belongings, I mean all my belongings. What I had left in my bedroom was my quilt and my pillows. I sold my studio couch, sold my TV, sold my wee video recorder, sold that. Sold everything and then I started selling some of my mum's stuff as well so I was really bad by this point.

(Sharon)

However, for the great majority of the addicts in our sample it quickly became impossible to sustain their addiction legitimately. The main problem was that their need for the drugs they were using increased as their tolerance level rose. This, in turn, inflated the amount of money they required to fund their habit. Perversely, since they tended to spend all that they had on drugs, success in obtaining money could lead to an increase in their consumption which, in turn, could lead to an even higher tolerance level and to the need for even more money. Eventually, all of the addicts in our study turned to illegitimate means to feed their habit. For the great majority, this meant theft or some other form of deception.

Our interviewees reported that, in support of their habit, they would have stolen anything from anyone and, as one said, 'not even think about it'. Any moral inhibitions as far as stealing was concerned were, it would appear, effectively de-activated by the overriding imperative to feed their habit. Quite simply, that was all that mattered. The addicts' own families

– parents, brothers or sisters – were frequent and ready targets for theft. In addition to money, anything else that was portable and sellable, like jewellery or cameras, would be taken. Money would also be borrowed and not repaid. However, most of the addicts' criminal activities were pursued outside the home, not for moral reasons but simply because only external sources could provide the sort of funds they required. Shoplifting was especially popular, particularly among the female addicts, while burglary, street theft and car crime were common sources of revenue for their male counterparts. In addition, a number of the male addicts supported their habit by dealing in drugs.

> Aye, I was dealing all sorts to feed my habit. I was dealing in everything. It didn't matter as long as I could make some money.
>
> *(Jimmy)*

For some of our sample, especially those for whom crime was a new experience, an initial resistance and apprehension might have to be overcome.

> Most of ma mates, they had all been in shoplifting and some of them had been in prison and, they were wide for everythin'. I was totally naïve . . . I wasn't brought up that way. I was brought up with morals and standards by ma family. But when you go into the drug scene you start to learn off the other boys and the lassies what they're doin'. They're shoplifting and I would never shoplift, I never had the bottle [nerve]. Even mad with drugs I couldn't do it. But the longer you get into them the more desperate you become, you'll start doin' it, you'll do anythin'.
>
> *(Stewart)*

In time, crime simply became a routine part of the addict's day. For some, it was almost a full-time activity occupying several hours each day, often seven days a week. As Lizzie put it, shoplifting to her 'was like a full-time job . . . it was nine in the morning 'till five at night, seven days a week'. Frequently, crimes would be committed while the addict was under the influence of drugs. This was often deliberate since many reported requiring the courage that the drug provided in order to be able to perpetrate the crime. On the other hand, though, being under the influence of drugs could impair the addicts' judgement and/or make them reckless, thereby increasing the risk of being caught.

I've got a previous of I think about fifteen charges, they're all theft from shops and stores and that. I mean, if I wasn't swallowing jellies, I'd be careful. But all these times I've been caught, without one exception at all, I've always been mad with it. I thought I was invisible. I mean I used to walk out of [supermarket] – this was before I started stealing dearer things that you made more money from – I used to walk out of there with the big giant jars of coffee, I'd have six of them round here, 20 packets of bacon all round and up this sleeve and maybe 20 packs there. I was like the fucking Michelin man walkin' out and I used to think I could get away with things like that . . . the reason I've always been caught has been through jellies or somethin'.

(Harry)

Committing crimes while under the influence of drugs could also mean that addicts might have no recollection of what they had done. As in Roy's case, this could lead to a number of rude awakenings.

You can't remember what you've done or anythin'. I mean I don't know how many times I've woken up in different police stations doin' weekenders. Havin' to go to court and I've not got a clue why I'm there.

(Roy)

Eight of the women reported turning to prostitution to fund their habit. It is important to record that this was not a positive choice on their part. Without exception, they hated it and only took it up out of desperation. All of the women who got involved in prostitution said that it was the last thing they wanted to do, or could imagine themselves doing, but at the time it was the only way in which they could obtain the sort of money they required to support their habit. Nearly all of them reported needing to be high on drugs in order to face what they had to do.

I was prostitutin' and basically I didn't like it. I was gettin' stoned out of my face to do it, but when I woke up straight in the morning I was like, 'Oh my God what am I doin'?' It made me lose total, whatever respect I had for myself.

(Mary)

Even then, some of the women found that they could not continue. Maggie, for example, only lasted a week.

I ended up meeting this other lassie from Possil and she was out on the street so she [said] to me 'come out on the street and you'll get the money for your drugs'. So I went out. I'll never forget it the first night. I don't know what made me go to the actual extent of actually goin' 'cos that was somethin' I never imagined myself doin'. That was the last resort kind of thing. So I went and I did it and I got fifteen pounds or somethin' like that and I just kept on doin' it but I only stayed on the street for about a week and I couldn't do it anymore.

(Maggie)

In the following account, Bridie chronicles the guilt, humiliation, danger and sense of revulsion that women endure when they turn to prostitution.

So eventually this friend of mine was . . . in a massage parlour at the time and she says well, y'know, this was how she was feeding her habit. And all the things I said I would never ever do, I did it. I used to say I would never get to that stage. If I got as bad as that I would stop. Then it's easier said than done . . . So I went for an interview in a massage parlour and . . . I thought it was like a talking interview. But I later learned the interview wasn't, his very words were he had to try me out to see if I was good enough. He paid me for it and I walked out of there and I felt so cheap and so dirty, but I was so tired of being arrested for shopliftin', I had nowhere else to turn, it was ma only means of money and basically the only thing in ma mind was drugs, gettin' money for the drugs. So I started in the massage parlour and he gave me money for a mini-skirt, suspenders and fake tan. And the fake tan was to cover up ma needle marks, but that was impossible. I had to wear long sleeves all the time. I couldn't wear T-shirts. Basically my kind of day when I was workin' was work all night, sleep durin' the day, wake up about five, take my drugs and out again to sell ma body. But the massage parlour didn't last long because the boss thought, he thought that because I worked for him he could have me anytime he liked so I couldn't put up with it. I expected a big handsome guy in a Porsche with Armani suits and whatever, tanned and all that but there he was standing in front of me this wee fat creep and he was [disgusting] and his hair was all greasy and everything and he made me sick he really did and I couldn't put up with him any longer so I took to the streets. I took beatings off the punters [clients]. A guy tried to strangle me one night in his car and I don't know how I got free but I did and from ma head to ma toes I was covered in bruises 'cos he'd set about me with a belt. I was all welt marks, ma breasts, in between ma legs, every-where. I was burnt with cigarettes . . . Basically it frightens you but it doesn't frighten you enough because again in your mind you're sayin', 'well I need to do this'. Basically all I was interested in was money for the drugs at the end of the day.

(Bridie)

She also goes on to describe in a touching way how her father, naïvely, offered to fund her habit in order to take her off the streets.

I was really sick of the kind of life I was leading and hurting ma family the way I was hurting them. And ma mother and father finding out I was sellin' ma body. Especially ma father to accept his daughter was doin' that, it's not very nice. I mean it was really heartbreakin'. So ma father said he'd be willing to feed ma habit to keep me off the streets but that was no use 'cos he didn't realise it was so dear [expensive]. He thought by givin' me £20 that would be it.

(Bridie)

According to our interviewees, living with addiction meant a life of deceit and manipulation, a life in which they would do anything to get drugs. Nearly all of them found themselves doing things they would not have contemplated doing prior to their addiction. For a high proportion of the addicts, their actions in support of their drug use led to imprison-ment. For many of them, this was regarded philosophically as being an occupational hazard.

I think it's always been in the back of ma mind that the last place I want to end up in is prison but if it happens it happens, there's nothin' you can do about it. You've just got to get your head down and get on with it I suppose.

(Fraser)

Another major occupational hazard was deteriorating health as a consequence of drug use. For the injecting users, serious vein damage was common and, of course, there was the ever-present risk of contracting HIV or hepatitis C. The ultimate health risk for all drug users was the danger of overdosing. However, for most of their drug-using career the health implications of their habit appeared to be of little significance to the addicts. Indeed, whether they lived or died became a matter of complete indifference to some of them.

> Basically you don't care if it happens to you, d'you know what I mean. I didn't care if I lived or died. I was going nowhere basically and that's just the way I thought. It never really crossed ma mind, I don't suppose you sat and thought about it and weighed it up or anything. Basically it was just somethin' that could happen and if it happened it happened.
>
> *(Sharon)*

It is likely that, for the overwhelming majority of addicts, the addict lifestyle contains within it the seeds of its own destruction. Some addicts die of overdoses or from health problems resulting from their drug use, some commit suicide and others meet their death through drug-related violence. However, the majority of addicts, including those in our sample, probably find their way out of addiction by other means and it is to them and their accounts of how they were able to beat the dragon of their addiction that we now turn.

3 Deciding to quit

This chapter examines the initial part of the process by which our interviewees overcame their addiction. Specifically, it is concerned with the decision to quit and the factors and circumstances which influenced that decision. How and for what reasons is the decision taken, why is it taken when it is and what factors encourage or impede its emergence? In other words, the chapter is about the *why* as opposed to the *how* of the process by which addicts escape from their addiction.

The decision to stop taking drugs is, of course, absolutely fundamental to any attempt at recovery. Although it carries no guarantee of success, it is nevertheless a decisive moment in any addict's career since, without it, it is unlikely that recovery will take place at all. In this chapter we explore the recovering addicts' own perceptions of how this decision was reached and the factors which influenced it. Specifically we examine the link between, on the one hand, the external reality and circumstances of the drug user's life and, on the other, the cognitive processes through which the decision to stop using occurs. While the literature on recovery from addiction identifies a range of experiences that correlate with the decision to give up drugs, we will argue that significant events, including changes in the addict's circumstances or in his or her social milieu, are not sufficient in themselves to explain why a successful decision to stop is made. As we will see, these objective conditions do not suddenly materialise out of the blue nor do they inevitably lead to a decision to quit. What has to be explained, therefore, is why it is that the external events and circumstances that are commonly associated with the decision to stop are effective when they are. Following Biernacki (1986), we will argue that the key to understanding this process and its timing lies in the way in which these events and circumstances are interpreted in relation to the individual's sense of self. Specifically, we will show that what motivates the addict to give up drugs is the way in which external events and circumstances reveal the unacceptable extent to which his or her identity has been damaged by addiction (McIntosh and McKeganey 2001).

Our analysis is conducted from a symbolic interactionist perspective. The key concept in symbolic interactionism is the notion of 'self'. This refers to how people see themselves or their sense of who and what they are – in other words, their identity. According to the symbolic interactionist approach, one's sense of self is continually formed and reformed through interaction with others, as individuals internalise the attitudes which others hold towards them (Mead 1934, Blumer 1969). However, the messages which are received from external sources are not incorporated automatically into the individual's sense of self. An important part of the process of maintaining and reforming one's identity lies in the individual's ability to interpret the messages which he or she receives from others and to accept, reject or modify them. In this chapter we examine the implications which the life as a drug addict had for the individual's sense of self and the role that this played in the decision to stop.

Addiction and identity

For our sample of recovering addicts, giving up drugs was not a single, once-and-for-all experience. On the contrary, the great majority had made several attempts to stop. Most of these, by definition, had been unsuccessful. This pattern of repeated episodes of abstinence and relapse is, according to the literature on de-addiction, a prominent feature of the biography of most drug addicts (Washton 1989, Klingemann 1994, Prins 1994).

When asked about their attempts to stop and what had influenced their decisions, our interviewees gave a variety of reasons which were, in range and content, consistent with those identified in the literature and, most commonly, included the following: the impact of their drug use on their partner, children or family; threats to one's health; to keep their partner or get a partner back; to prevent their children being removed from them; a sense of weariness with the routine and demands involved in maintaining their drug use; the death of someone close due to drugs; and the threat of prison as a result of criminal activities engaged in to support their habit. However, what is striking in these accounts is that the experiences and events which our respondents cited as reasons for stopping did not, on the face of it, appear to differ in type or quality as far as successful and unsuccessful attempts were concerned. The same sorts of reasons were given for both.

This immediately raises the question of how we can account for our addicts' eventual success in exiting drug misuse. What was it that distinguished their latest, and apparently successful, attempt from their earlier unsuccessful ones? Are the events and circumstances surrounding the two different in important respects or is there some other factor at work? On the basis of our interviews with the recovering addicts, we believe that there is another factor and that this element has to do with the addict's sense of identity. Our data suggest that what distinguishes successful attempts is that they have at their core a concern with the individual's sense of self. More specifically, we will argue, they are stimulated by a desire to restore what has been described by Goffman as a 'spoiled identity' (Goffman 1963). Goffman characterises a spoiled or stigmatised identity as follows:

> The central feature of the stigmatised individual's situation in life can now be stated. It is a question of what is often, if vaguely, called 'acceptance'. Those who have dealings with him fail to accord him the respect and regard which the un-contaminated aspects of his social identity have led them to anticipate extending, and have led him to anticipate receiving; he echoes this denial by finding that some of his own attributes warrant it. (Goffman 1963, p. 19)

In other words, the central feature of a spoiled identity is the realisation by an individual that he or she exhibits characteristics that are unacceptable both to him or herself and to significant others. This realisation was very evident in the accounts provided by our recovering addicts. In describing their eventual exit from drug misuse and the conditions and circumstances surrounding it, the theme which dominates our interviewees' accounts is their concern to repair an identity severely damaged by drugs and to recapture a sense of value and self-respect; in other words, a desire to regain a positive sense of self. Whereas earlier attempts to abstain tend to be utilitarian in nature and geared to achieving a particular practical outcome – such as getting one's partner to return or avoiding losing one's children – what characterises the successful attempt to exit is a fundamental questioning and rejection of what one has become, together with a desire and resolution to change. It is important to note, however, that we are not claiming that a desire to restore one's identity was a sufficient condition for successful exit from drug misuse; that this on its own would guarantee success. This was clearly not the case since, as we will see, there were instances where even this resolve did not work. Rather, what we are suggesting is that the sort of cognitive shift that we have described comes close to being a *necessary* condition for such change to occur.

We should make it clear that only a minority of our interviewees referred explicitly to a desire to restore a spoiled identity as being at the heart of their decision to quit. More commonly, they would make oblique and implicit reference to the notion and importance of a degraded sense of self and to their perceived need to do something about it. What is more important, however, is that references to a spoiled identity – whether direct or indirect – were a feature of nearly all of our respondents' descriptions of their successful attempts at recovery.

The importance of identity was perhaps expressed most directly in the notion, articulated by a substantial number (23) of our interviewees, that you could only exit drug misuse successfully if you did it 'for yourself'. What they meant by this was that you would be unlikely to succeed if you sought to stop for the sake of others – for example, because of the effect your drug use was having on your children – or if you abstained in order to obtain a pragmatic goal, such as getting a girlfriend to return. Success would only come if you did it for yourself, for your self-respect and sense of worth; in short, if you did it for the sake of your own identity. The following extracts provide a powerful illustration of this view. For Maria, the key to successful recovery was her desire 'to be somebody' and to acquire a feeling of 'self-respect and self-worth' while for Joe it was 'doin' it for myself'.

Q   Why is it important to clean up for yourself as opposed to the kids?

R   Because I'm the only one that can give myself self-respect and I couldn't give that to myself when I was a user because I didn't think enough of myself when I was a user. An' I knew I could come off drugs 'cause I've already done it and I did have a wee bit of self-respect then but it was like I didn't really want to be clean. I wanted to be clean for the bairns [children]. I wanted the bairns back, and I thought the only way I'm going to get the bairns back is if I'm clean and I think that's how I mucked up the last time. Because I wasn't really wanting to be clean, 'cause I liked using. Whereas this time it was like I wanted to be clean, I want to be somebody, I don't want to be a user. I want to be a normal person an' I want things that other people's got, like confidence and self-respect and self-worth in yourself.

(Maria)

Well a couple of times I did try to stop for different reasons, like I tried to stop because ma mum was goin' to throw me out of the house or because ma sister wasn't talking to me or because ma girlfriend had left me or because I was going to get the sack [from] ma job. But basically what was happening there was I was doing it all for the wrong reasons. I wasn't doin' it for myself and it is the only way it works if you do it for yourself because all the answers lie within.

(Joe)

Kate also linked her recovery quite explicitly to her desire to rebuild her identity.

R   I think it had to come from me, you know what I mean. Not because of the wean [child] or because of this or because of that, for me.

Q   What do you mean for you?

R   Well for me as a person wantin' to be straight an' sayin' I'm not just a junkie an' I'm not in the gutter, I'm a person the same as you.

The crucial element here is the distinction between deciding to be a non-addict and stopping for other reasons. The problem with the latter is that part of the addict still wants to use drugs; in other words, it is not that they want to give up drugs but, merely, that doing so will help them to achieve some other desirable goal. According to our interviewees, the key to a successful exit from drug use was to stop because you no longer wanted to be a user; in short, to do it because you wanted to change your self.

One of the problems with stopping for other reasons is that the drug is frequently, perhaps usually, considerably more powerful than a whole range of very good reasons for stopping. Certainly, for Angela and Laura, the power of the drug could only too readily even override consideration for their children's welfare.

> The bit of me that wanted to stay on was saying fuck the bairns, look after yourself, just never mind the bairns, the bairns are all right, the bairns have got clothes, the bairns'll get fed. Whereas in actual fact they weren't, it's mind games, it's quite scary.
>
> *(Angela)*

> I had ma wee boy an' I knew I was destroying his life an' I felt helpless but there was still a wee part of me that wanted to be his mother an' be responsible for him an' all that stuff. He was doing everything for himself, just like a grown-up at four years old, so grown up, it just made me feel, 'Oh he's OK he doesn't need me'. There's just always that wee bit of you wants to come off but it's just, I don't know, I just feel it's dead powerful the drug itself, it's just so powerful. It haunts you everywhere you go, every step further you get it hauls you three steps back. I just felt dead helpless sometimes.
>
> *(Laura)*

According to many of our recovering addicts you only had a realistic prospect of overcoming this power when it was the drug-using identity that was being rejected.

While a proportion of our interviewees made a fairly explicit link between their sense of self and their decision to quit, the majority of them referred to the significance and role of identity somewhat less directly. For example, for many, the negative impact which their lives as drug addicts had had upon their sense of self was reported in the form of a deep unhappiness with the sort of people they had become. This was expressed in a variety of ways. For instance, Angela – a drug user for nine years and an addict for six – described her unhappiness in terms of having no self-respect and a sense of self-loathing. In the following extract, she repeatedly refers to 'hating' aspects of her life as an addict as well as 'hating' herself.

> I was really sick of life revolving around drugs an' sick of the things I would do to get drugs . . . an' just sick of drugs bein' the

main thing in life. Drugs came before anything, they came before myself, the house, ma family. And just the culture, I hated the folk I was with as well, I hated the folk that I was associatin' with, the lifestyle. But I would still do it because I was gettin' the drugs. I hated the lyin' and the cheatin', sleepin' with folk I didn't like because they had drugs on them, and I just hated havin' no self-respect . . . I really hated myself. I really hated the junkie . . . and I hated havin' to use ma body to get drugs, I really hated that, a feeling of disgust really, disgusted with myself and the feeling of desperation. I really hated feeling desperate for drugs. It's like the only thing that was right at the front of ma mind was drugs, where am I goin' to get this, where am I goin' to get that. Whereas in actual fact I should've been thinking, what am I goin' to give the bairn for his breakfast, his lunch and his tea, what's he doin', who's he out playing with.

(Angela)

Fiona described her unhappiness with herself in terms of not being able to 'look other people in the eye' and having no self-respect. She issues the plea that, now that she has recovered, she should be 'taken seriously as a human being'.

And the answer to your question is what made me do it [give up drugs] . . . because the day you throw your poison down the [toilet] is the day you stand back on earth and look other people in the eye and say, I am not a drug addict, I am better. I have recovered, I have fought it. I am better now, please take me seriously as a human being.

(Fiona)

Steve summed up his sense of disgust with himself by describing his addict persona as that of a 'bastard'.

I saw the ways I was going to get money to get drugs an' I didn't like it . . . shoplifting. I was breaking in, lots o' sick things. I would rip off anybody. Someone would give me their trust and that's me, I've ripped them off kind of thing. Like somebody would give me a loan of money and I wouldn't pay them back. There was hundreds o' these scams. Nobody trusted [me] anymore, know what I mean? I didn't trust myself anymore, I was sick bein' a bastard, that's what I was, one big bastard.

(Steve)

Sometimes the addicts' sense of revulsion at what they had become was linked to the belief that, during the period of their addiction, they had become different from the people they felt themselves to be 'at heart'. In other words, their addiction had prevented them from expressing what they felt to be their true selves. For Nancy and Sammy, for instance, it amounted to not recognising the people they had become.

I didn't recognise the person I was . . . I was just a nippy horrible person that fought with everybody, didn't have a kind word for anybody, spoke to people as if they were absolute dirt an' I wasn't really in a position to speak to anybody in that manner. I'd totally lost it. The person I'd turned into was just totally unbelievable.

(Nancy)

Aye there was a lot o' times I wanted to end it because I knew I wasn't that person, I didn't recognise the person I was.

(Sammy)

Callum expressed the belief that his addiction had distorted his personal development.

I was weighing up drug use and my purpose in life kind of thing. I wasn't put here for drugs . . . I'm not here just for that. I don't know but I just thought there was something better here for me rather than the years I've been through. Because I don't think my true character ever developed because I was that young that my character just had no chance to develop. Getting into drugs at such a young age, I think it put a blocker see. I think I'm a different person than what I would have been if I hadn't got into drugs at an early age I'm most certain of that.

(Callum)

As the preceding extracts imply, while the addicts' sense of self was undoubtedly radically altered by their addiction and drug-using lifestyle, a memory of their former drug-free selves nevertheless remained. Our study suggests that this residual identity often played a vital role in the decision to quit. First, this sense of their former selves enabled the addicts, through comparison, to recognise the extent to which their identities had been damaged by their addiction. Second, the memory of their former selves also contained seeds of hope for the future because it enshrined within it the basis for believing that they did not have to be the people that they had become; they had been different in the past and could be so again. In other words, their residual identities both reinforced the need for change and, at the same time, revealed the potential for it. The role which their residual identities played in their decision to give up drugs can be seen in the following extracts.

> I wanted ma life back, I wanted to be normal, I didn't know what that meant but you knew you had had a reasonably normal life an' you said this isn't right, I shouldn't be like this.
>
> *(Alison)*

> I wanted to try it [giving up drugs] because when I had that gap from 13 to about 17 I had a really good life, I enjoyed maself and I wanted it to be like that again and I wanted to make somethin' of ma life again and that's when I decided there must be more to me than this.
>
> *(Mary)*

Although they expressed it in different ways and with differing degrees of explicitness, what is common to our addicts' accounts of their successful decision to quit is the recognition that their drug-using identity was no longer acceptable and had to change. This identity, they believed, was associated with a lifestyle that allowed individuals no room for self-respect and, indeed, had corrupted their true selves. For our addicts, it was this sense of a spoiled identity, in combination with an unwillingness or inability to live with it any longer, which led to the decision to stop using. The cost of continuing had simply become too great as far as their sense of self was concerned.

Reflections of one's self

When asked to account for their decision to give up drugs, our recovering addicts would generally refer to a range of precipitating circumstances and events. As we indicated earlier, these might include such things as: a desire to re-establish a relationship with a partner; the impact of their drug use on those close to them; an attempt to prevent the removal of their children; threats to their health and so on. While these 'reasons' for quitting were important, our analysis of our interviewees' accounts suggests that the influence of these experiences was indirect. In short, these events and circumstances were seldom, if ever, sufficient in themselves to promote permanent exit from drug misuse although, as we will see later, they could provide the impetus for temporary abstinence. Their potential effect was mediated by the meaning which the individuals ascribed to them and the implications which these interpretations had for their sense of self. Insofar as they contributed to the decision to give up drugs, these experiences did so by revealing to the addicts the nature and extent of their spoiled identity and by forcing them to review what they had become. In essence, they acted as a mirror to the self. We base this interpretation on the fact that our interviewees' accounts of the effect that these experiences had on their decision to give up drugs nearly always referred to the way in which they influenced how they saw and felt about themselves. More importantly, however, they did so in a way that suggested that this is where their real significance lay.

The circumstances which forced the addicts to review their identities could be single events or ongoing experiences or, frequently, a combination of both. First, it is clear that ongoing aspects of the drug-using lifestyle could exert a powerful influence upon how the individuals saw themselves. In many cases, it was the impact which their drug use was having on those close to them that forced the addicts to confront what they had become. For example, Glen and Angela reported feeling a profound sense of guilt at what their behaviour and lifestyle were doing to their families.

> I think the main thing that got me off it was basically seein' the bairn growing up. Seein' the hurt in ma ex-wife's eyes. I never even realised what I had done, seein' the hurt in her eyes. Becomin' involved in drugs and really, livin' on the bare essentials. I would take every penny so I could score drugs and leave her with practically nothin'. Her and the bairn.
>
> *(Glen)*

> Ma house was a mess, folk comin' to ma house at all hours, folk havin' parties in ma house. It was disgustin', the lifestyle was

disgustin' and it was scary as well because the wee boy was with me and he was seein' everythin' that was going on round about him as well, and that's the scary bit about that.

(Angela)

Jane recounted how having to buy a uniform for her daughter in instalments brought home to her the cost of her addiction for others.

...ma wee lassie she's wantin' her brownie uniform and I was buying her somethin' every week. If I wasn't a junkie I'd be able to go out and buy her the full thing at once. So you've got all this guilt that you're goin' an' buying somethin' every week 'cos you've got to keep so much for yourself. It's hard tryin' to explain to your wee lassie.

(Jane)

For some individuals, the measures which they had to adopt in order to acquire the money needed to support their habit provided one of the primary sources of their disgust with themselves. For Brian it was stealing from those close to him that was his greatest source of regret. As he implies in the following extract, this made him feel totally diminished as a person.

I was stealing out of the house. My mam noticed that, stealing out of her purse and things, stealing out of my girlfriend's purse. We'd just got a house together, stealing out of the house. We'd got engaged and we'd had an engagement party. She noticed things were going missing from that, our engagement stuff. I was stealing stuff out of that to earn quick money for a hit. My mam barred me out of her house. Got barred from my mam's house. Got kicked out by my girlfriend. My girlfriend fell out with me for the first time. I felt like shit. I felt that size.

(Brian)

For Mary it was her prostitution that emphasised how low she had sunk.

Basically I couldn't live with it. I didn't work the streets for a long time, I worked the streets for six weeks but that was long enough for me to feel really shitty about myself. Basically I would have done anythin' for the money and that was just pure degradin' myself. But at the time you're so stoned you don't care. But if you wake up straight in the morning you go 'God I've got to do the same all over again'. And that was the final straw for me. That was my lowest point . . . I would have done anything for money.

(Mary)

The process of recognising and acknowledging a spoiled identity and the subsequent decision to give up drugs were usually the result of a gradual process of realisation as opposed to a 'road to Damascus' type of conversion. Our interviewees indicated that the decision to quit could develop over a period of months or even years. As Ian reported, 'I suppose I'd been thinking about it [giving up drugs] for a couple of years but just couldn't bring myself to do it.' Over time, and with continuing exposure to events and circumstances which challenged their drug-using identity, the addicts gradually reached the conclusion that they could no longer tolerate what they had become and therefore had to change. Certainly, a substantial number of the addicts in our sample had, as we shall see, what could be described as rock bottom experiences which led to a profound questioning of their sense of self. However, these episodes did not arise out of the blue and, instead, were usually the end point of an evolving process of awareness and of a succession of attempts to come to terms with a spoiled identity.

Most commonly, the addict's recognition of how far they had deteriorated, and their attendant resolve to change, derived from the simple accumulation of a variety of negative messages. Sometimes, though, this process was accelerated, or brought to a head, by the occurrence of certain dramatic events. In common with other studies in the area (such as Stimson and Oppenheimer 1982, Waldorf and Biernacki 1981, Shaffer 1992), we found that the decision to quit was often precipitated by certain 'trigger' events. These frequently, though not always, took the form of something fairly major such as the death or departure of a partner or, as in the following example, the birth of a child. In the following extract, Malky, who had been a heroin addict for about 12 years, recounts the experience of having received a note from a relative informing him of the birth of his daughter.

'Diane has just given birth to your daughter', 'know like that. So I crumpled it up, threw it down, went out, got a bottle o' jellies with about twenty in it, got myself works, went up to the bathroom and stood there. I was like that. I had the bottle here and a set of works. At that minute it was like a set of scales in my hand . . . I put the works over to the side. I said to myself, 'Do you want what you've lost or do you want to keep on going with this?' Just a really weird feeling in that bathroom. What I did was, burst all the jellies, threw them all down the toilet, snapped the spike off the works, put that down the toilet, had a wash, pulled out some clothes, put them on and went right up to the hospital. Walked into the hospital, walked right into where Diane and the bairn was. Her family was there and my family. They just all sort of looked around . . . I just walked across but the feeling was like rejection, it was like they were all cringing at me being there, standing there, know. It was like they just hated me, the presence of me. So I said 'see you later', looked at the bairn, walked out to the foyer and I picked up the phone. I said 'Grandad this is Malky, I need help.'

(Malky)

For Brian it was the death of his partner that proved decisive.

They said, 'We found Alice dead an hour ago in your toilet.' Know what I mean and that was through drugs. I nearly died. I still remember that moment, 'cos that did me in. I wasn't mad in love with the lassie, she was good to me, I liked her. That was the turning point. I don't know what it was, it was somethin' inside me just changed. My whole attitude changed. I didn't even have a hit that day, I went the whole day without a hit.

(Brian)

For Bridie, an injecting drug user for 11 years, it was a warning from her doctor that her life was in danger that acted as the trigger for her to quit.

The doctor told me straight, you've not got a chance in hell, stop this, if you don't you're goin' to have to get your leg amputated and eventually it will be death. I was really frightened.

(Bridie)

What these events did was to bring the addicts up short and suddenly throw their lives into sharp relief, highlighting how problematic their addiction had become and/or forcing them to recognise the extent to which their identities had become degraded. However, while trigger events may have provided the necessary catalyst for some addicts' decisions to quit, our interviewees' accounts suggest that these dramatic moments typically occurred at the end of a period within which a range of other events and circumstances had already forced the individuals to undertake a critical review of their lifestyles and the people they had become. In other words, for most of the addicts the trigger came at the end of a period of reflection and review that had been going on for some time. In that sense, these events probably simply brought to a head a process that was evolving anyway.

It is important to recognise that the experiences and events that prompted the addicts to review their identities could be either positive or negative. The former could include things like the birth of a child or, as in the following example, the beginning of a new relationship.

> As I say, I met Jackie, and eventually I could see something in the future. I don't know what it was, I was just a lot happier. As I say, it was only a girlfriend at the time but I didn't like usin' her like that because I knew there was something special with her, know. And . . . I started to see somethin' in the future rather than just worrying about a bit of jag and whatever I had to batter [use] that night and not worry about tomorrow. I just wanted to be as good to Jackie I suppose as she was to me, treat her with a bit of respect I think. I think that's what it was. Obviously I fell in love, that's got a lot to do with it.
>
> *(Alistair)*

The latter comprised things like the poor condition of one's children, the fear of having them removed, the break-up of a relationship, the deteriorating health of the addict or, as in Steve's case, the death of a friend due to drugs.

> There was people dyin' all around us, best friends, I had buried about thirteen people, lowered thirteen coffins, been to about twenty funerals from drug overdoses and people dyin' from AIDS. My best friend died of the HIV virus and two weeks before his brother had just taken an overdose and that's what made it sink in, seein' people in the hospital and lyin' there dead and buryin' them. That freaked us out and I saw myself that way. I actually dreamt of my funeral, saw myself dyin' and that freaked me out.
>
> *(Steve)*

Both types of experience were important but in slightly different ways. While negative experiences and events served to illustrate the way in which the individual's identity had been damaged, the positive happenings in the addict's life provided a vision of an alternative future and reinforced the advantages of a drug-free lifestyle.

The illustrations presented in this section not only highlight the role of key circumstances and events in promoting change, more particularly they reinforce the centrality of identity in the decision-making process. The significance of these key experiences and events lay not so much in the fact that they were unacceptable to the addicts but much more in what they revealed to individuals about their situation and how they made them feel about themselves and the sort of people they had become.

A gradual process

Perhaps one of the reasons why the process of deciding to give up drugs is, perforce, a gradual and evolving one is because it involves the individual accepting a negative definition of him or herself. The symbolic interactionist literature shows clearly that the imposition of a negative definition of the self will be resisted for as long as possible because of its implications for the individual's sense of worth. From the perspective of symbolic interactionism, our identities, or concepts of self, are formed largely on the basis of the innumerable social encounters in which we are involved in the course of our lives and, in particular, by the views and reactions of others (Mead 1934, Blumer 1969). These influences can include events with social significance as well as interactions with others. In other words, the way in which we think of ourselves, our sense of self, is shaped by the people and events with whom we interact, with these interactions, and the messages which they contain, having the power to confirm or alter our identities. However, the communications and signals which we receive are not simply absorbed and internalised in an automatic and unquestioning way. On the contrary, these inputs are subject to challenge and interpretation by the individual. In consequence, they may be either accepted by the individual in their entirety, partially incorporated within one's sense of self or rejected completely.

Within this interpretative process, there is likely to be considerable resistance on the part of the individual to the imposition of a negative view of self. This, we suggest, is why it takes time, and frequently something dramatic, for drug users to come to accept that their identity has been spoiled. This acceptance usually comes at the point at which the array of negative messages about one's behaviour can no longer be denied or rationalised. It is simply no longer possible for the addict to see his or her lifestyle and identity in anything other than a negative way. Indeed, one of the main actions of trigger events may be to provide the final straw which forces this acknowledgement.

The addicts' eventual acceptance of their spoiled identities was facilitated by the fact that this recognition was not an entirely negative experience. The acceptance of an unfavourable view of themselves was always balanced by a desire to change and to build a different future. In this way, their recognition of what they had become could be regarded by them as a positive step on the road to new, more favourable, identities. It is likely that the belief that change was possible, and that their identities could be restored, was an essential element in the cognitive shift involved in the decision to give up drugs. Without the hope of a more positive future, acceptance of their spoiled identities would have been, at the very least, much more difficult.

Future orientation

As the foregoing discussion implies, the recognition that one's identity has been spoiled is not sufficient on its own to promote the decision to give up drugs. An important corollary of this realisation is a desire for a new identity and a different style of life. It was clear from our addicts' accounts of their decision to come off drugs that the two things – the recognition of a spoiled identity and the vision of a renewed future – went hand in hand. In describing their decision, our respondents made frequent references to their aspiration both to restore their identities and to achieve a better future and it was clear that they saw each as being dependent on the other. For example, Bernadette presented her hopes for the future in terms of her desire to be 'normal' and to fulfil normal ambitions.

> I wanted a future ... I knew that I couldn't sort of go about the way I was doing. I wasn't happy, I mean I wanted to be normal. I wanted to have the likes of just a house and eventually get

married, and have a job. I was kind of burnt out. My mind was just burnt out. I was seeing other people outside. My pals I'd started goin' back about with again. I was seein' them going on holidays and things like that, having nice clothes and things like that when I was just still bumming about.

(Bernadette)

Scott wanted to repair the damage of nine years of addiction and to catch up on lost opportunities.

I knew I had enough of it . . . I was nine years on them; it was destroyin' me . . . I'd done a lot of damage. I realised that I wanted to go and do something. Go and get a job, do things I wanted to do years ago but I never done.

(Scott)

The addicts' vision of an alternative future did not appear out of a void. It was usually prompted and reinforced by the same events and circumstances which revealed the flaws in their drug-using identity and lifestyle. For example, the effect which their behaviour was having on those close to them not only revealed the depths to which they had descended, but also suggested an alternative way of life which would avoid such harm. Frequently, though, the desirability of a lifestyle free of drugs was stimulated by a positive occurrence such as the beginning of a new relationship or the arrival of a new baby. Such events re-awakened the addict's perspective on the future and, in particular, demonstrated that it could be better than the present and that it was something worth striving for. In other words, these glimpses of an alternative, and more desirable, future – whatever their origins – were a vital component of the addict's motivation to change his or her lifestyle and give up drugs.

There is, however, one further and very important aspect to this. For the cognitive shift which we have described to take place, it is not enough for addicts to perceive a new identity and a new life as being desirable. They also have to believe that this is *feasible*. Without this, any inclination to alter one's behaviour will swiftly evaporate. It is with the addict's conviction that an alternative life course is possible that the deterministic aspect of the drug career is removed and there is some point to the individual attempting to change. In short, it is vital that addicts believe that there is a realisable alternative to what they have become and that they can realistically aspire to a life free of drugs.

The role of unsuccessful attempts to stop

Nearly all of our interviewees could recount tales of previous attempts to stop taking drugs which had ended in failure. The periods of abstinence which they reported varied from a matter of days to two or three years. As we observed earlier, these relapses were usually associated with attempts to come off drugs which did not involve an accompanying desire on the part of the addict to change his or her identity. However, there is good reason to believe that these failed attempts are not simply a waste of time and that they may play a highly significant role in the process of recovery. Our study suggests that there are at least two respects in which periods of abstinence may assist in this process, in both instances by reinforcing the decision to stop by linking it to the addict's sense of self.

First, for some addicts, a period of freedom from drug use clarifies and highlights the extent to which their identities have been damaged by drugs. There are two aspects to this.

1 During abstinence, addicts' lives as users are thrown into sharp relief when set against the backdrop of their new, drug-free lifestyles and they are able to see more clearly the depths to which they had sunk. In other words, it is easier for them to perceive the full extent of the degradation occasioned by their addiction when the drug-using life-style can be viewed from the perspective of a non-user.

2 A period of abstinence allows the addict's residual identity to re-emerge and for comparisons to be made between it and his or her drug-using persona. Such comparisons with this former, non-using identity and lifestyle can have a powerful impact on the addict and can strengthen considerably their resolution to change. For example, Peter acquired a sense of a different future as a result of enforced abstinence due to imprisonment.

> See with my dealing I kept gettin' turned over, busted, and got put into [prison] and that's the first break like from when I first started takin' barbiturates, that I had like total abstinence ... that's when I started thinkin' to myself ... what's been goin' on the past couple of years that I've missed out on.
>
> *(Peter)*

For Catriona, abstinence led to the rediscovery of a positive sense of herself.

Do you mean like what made me keep comin' back to try to come off? 'Cos I feel like I'm worth more now, whereas before I didn't have any respect for myself and I couldn't see myself bein' off drugs. That was life. But I had a taste for it and I liked bein' drug-free, there was things about me I didn't even know existed. I started to like wee bits about maself, you know what I mean, and when I was takin' drugs you just lose all that, you just go right down, and I wanted all that back . . . once I'd been drug-free for that ten month and used again I realised that I'd lost all that, you know what I mean. I hated maself for usin' drugs.

(Catriona)

Second, during abstinence, the addict acquires first-hand experience of the alternative life and identity to which he or she might aspire.

. . . like what happened to me once, I did get off and I was stayin' in Glasgow and I was off for what, four months. I started to go about with like ma pals that I'd grew up with in the street . . . that never used. And great, I was gettin' ma life back together again.

(Bernadette)

This serves to reinforce not only the desirability of a drug-free lifestyle but also, and equally importantly, its feasibility. If the addict can abstain from drug-taking for a time, why not for good?

The changing effect of the drug

In addition to the cognitive and perceptual shifts which occur in addicts and in their orientation towards their drug-taking, important changes also take place in the pharmacological effects of the drug over the period of addiction. Our study suggests that these latter changes play a major part in the addict's decision to stop using. In particular, there comes a time when all that taking the drug does is to allow the addict to maintain a minimum level of functioning. In other words, it merely enables the addict to feel normal. Simultaneously, the pleasurable effects of the drug gradually recede and the company of other users begins to lose its attraction. In short, after a time, drug-taking ceases to be pleasurable and the life stops being fun. A number of other researchers have drawn attention to the significance of this process in the decision to quit (Stimson and Oppenheimer 1982, Frykholm 1985, Prins 1994) and it was quite clear from our interviewees' accounts of their exit from drug misuse that this was an observation that they would endorse.

> That's the problem with drugs. You take them at the beginnin' and they make you feel great, know, nothin' affects you and then after a few months you're takin' the same amount and they don't do anythin' for you, they just make you feel like an empty person. At the beginnin' you feel like the best there is and then in the end you take them to feel the best you possibly can. The way you and I are sittin' now, a lot of people take drugs every morning just to feel the way you and I do now which is completely normal. Not stoned, not intoxicated, just normal.
>
> *(Jimmy)*

> You got out, got your drugs, went home and that was you, you know, you just couldn't function without them. At first it was great. Oh it was marvellous. When you first start takin' them you're on top of the world, nothin' can be bad, everythin' is great to you, shiny, happy, people. It's just . . . then it gets the better of you and you don't even get a buzz out of it after a while. Basically you're just takin' it to feel normal and that's no use. That's what made me really decide in the end to start the reduction. 'Cos I wasn't feelin' it, takin' 50 mills a day and I wasn't feelin' any different, I was just feelin' normal, so I'm sayin' to myself, 'what's the point in this I might as well be off it. I mean, I'm not gettin' anythin' out of it anymore.'
>
> *(Bill)*

When the drug and its associated lifestyle lose their appeal, the business of acquiring and administering it also takes on a different perspective and meaning for the addict. It would appear from the literature that, for most addicts, the stage is reached when the process of obtaining and taking drugs comes to be regarded as a tedious, pleasureless and almost tyrannical activity (e.g. Biernacki 1986). The addicts in our sample described similar feelings. Many recalled a tiredness or weariness with the life and a sense of being 'burned out'.

> At that time I'd just had enough. I'd been sick that many times, withdrawals, the whole humdrum routine, goin' out to score

every day, havin' a monkey on your back all the time. I'd been through all the shit all over the world for ten years. Ten years I thought to myself, oh fuck this, you're not goin' to get back into this again. Go back to your own hometown, get yourself straight.

(Frank)

I felt this was controlling my life or something like that anyway ... I think perhaps as the novelty wore off, y'know I think I just got bored. I'd had enough of the whole situation really ...

(Helen)

A particularly onerous feature of the drug-using routine was the problem which every addict had in financing his or her habit. In addition, though, the rising costs of an escalating habit also frequently led the addicts towards behaviours which were increasingly unacceptable to them, especially where they involved theft or prostitution.

The change that takes place in the pharmacological effect of the drug is, we would argue, an important pre-condition for a successful decision to stop. In other words, it is likely that, for most users, the potential for exit from drugs is heavily dependent upon drug-taking no longer being regarded as a pleasurable or attractive activity. Up to this point in the addicts' careers, the easier and more attractive option is to continue using. However, the realisation that the drug is no longer a positive presence in their lives – that it is no longer their friend – is an important turning point. Continuing to take the drug now involves substantial costs but without the compensating benefits. Instead of being their servant, it has become their master.

Now, it might be thought that once this point was reached it would be a relatively straightforward matter for the addict to stop using. Unfortunately, it is not quite that simple. The problem is that, while the positive effects of drug-taking may have evaporated, the physiological dependence remains and this continues to constitute a major barrier to any attempt at recovery. It is important at this juncture to distinguish between *wanting* and *needing* to take drugs, where wanting is the desire for the pleasurable effects and needing is a response to physiological dependence. While, in time, the addict may cease to derive any positive benefit or pleasure from drug-taking (the wanting), the physical dependence (the needing) remains to be conquered. As we will see, the fear of this process and the extreme discomfort which accompanies it is, for the great majority of users, a major impediment to change.

Rational decisions and rock bottom experiences

Much of the literature on routes out of drug misuse claims that the decision to quit is usually preceded by a profound emotional crisis of some sort. As we noted in Chapter 1, this experience is variously described as an 'existential crisis', an 'epistemological shift' or, most commonly, as hitting 'rock bottom'. All of these notions refer to the situation in which addicts arrive at a point in their drug-using careers beyond which they feel they cannot go. It is the stage at which the addict feels he or she must either give up drugs or face psychological and/or physical destruction. In other words, they have reached a point of no return.

As we reported earlier, for some writers, this type of experience is an essential step on the road to recovery from addiction. However, our study did not confirm this observation. While it was certainly true that, for a substantial proportion of the addicts in our sample, the decision to stop using was associated with a crisis or with what could be termed a rock bottom experience, this was not universal nor did it appear to be a necessary condition for a successful exit from drug misuse. In this sense, our findings are much closer to those of Biernacki (1986) who, on the basis of his research on spontaneous recovery from opiate addiction, identifies two principal routes out of drug use. One of these is the rock bottom type of experience referred to in the literature on recovery, the other exit route he describes as being based on 'rational decisions'. Biernacki argues that, while some addicts undergo a rock bottom experience from which the only alternative to rehabilitation is destruction, others exit on the basis of a less dramatic decision-making process. According to Biernacki (1986), 'Many addicts come to a point in their lives where they rationally and explicitly decide to stop using opiates. Often this point occurs after a cumulation of negative experiences coupled with some particularly significant and disturbing personal event' (p. 49). He continues, 'Some addicts . . . resolve to change their lives and stop using opiates when the option of continuing to use drugs entails consequences that are simply far too undesirable in terms of the view they have of themselves and their future lives. At this point, they rationally weigh each possibility and decide that they have much more to gain by breaking the addiction than by continuing it' (p. 53).

Both exit routes – rational decisions and rock bottom experiences – were clearly evident in our addicts' descriptions of the processes through which they gave up drugs. Thirty of them indicated quite clearly that they had decided to quit following a rock-bottom type crisis. At this stage, the addict feels that he or she has deteriorated to such an extent physically, socially and psychologically that there are only three possibilities open to them:

1   The addict can continue to use drugs but the result will be the total degradation of his or her identity and, probably, physical destruction as well.

2   The addict can attempt to exit through suicide. This option is given serious consideration by many users at this stage and is actually attempted by some.

3   The addict can try to break his or her addiction and thereby exit his or her drug-using career.

By the time they reach rock bottom, for many addicts, perhaps even most, the third option becomes the only realistic or acceptable alternative open to them. It is almost literally a case of do or die.

> Q   The time you did manage to come off, what do you think set that time apart from the other times to make it successful?

> R   Oh it was either that or just call a halt to ma life. I couldn't go on livin' that way I was livin' so it was one way or the other. Either succeed or totally give up and just take the whole bottle.
>
> *(Alison)*

A number of different elements can be discerned in our recovering addicts' descriptions of their rock bottom experiences. Prominent among these are: concerns with their health; a profound weariness with the demands of sustaining their habit; and a recognition that, if they continue, they will die. However, once again, a recurrent theme is the notion of a desperately degraded sense of self. Indeed, for many addicts the rock bottom experience is probably best characterised as a profound identity crisis. For example, Stewart described his rock bottom experience in terms of having reached his 'personal gutter' and having 'nobody to look down on'. For him, the alternative to quitting was to overdose.

> At the end I wanted to pack it in, it was either that or I was goin' to die. Just OD, sometimes you just wanted to die, not wake up.

We call it a personal gutter when you've just had enough. Some people it can be one year, two year, three year, some can be ten year, some people never ever get to it, they just don't want to face up to it. We call it a personal gutter because you always look down on people, you always compare yourself to somebody else that's lower down than you and unfortunately you end up down in the gutter yourself and there's nobody to look down on. You need to start looking up again and we call that a personal gutter. People have to hit that.

(Stewart)

Rhona also described her nadir in terms of believing that she could not sink any lower than she had. She had also reached the 'gutter'.

It was just desperation as I said, I just hit rock bottom . . . I think to come off drugs you've got to think you can't go any lower, that you believe you're right in the gutter an' you can't go any lower than what you are . . . I thought I couldn't go any lower than what I was an' I went to the doctor and he put me to the DPS and I was put on methadone.

(Rhona)

Having said that, though, in the majority of our interviewees' descriptions of the rock bottom experience, the physical, social and psychological consequences of their addiction came together to depict a state of degradation and despair which affected every aspect of their being. This tangled combination of elements can be seen clearly in the following extracts. For example, for Mary, fear of death and a very negative sense of self – 'nobody would talk to me, nobody liked me, I didn't like maself' – combined in her decision to stop.

But when I really decided I wanted to clean up, basically my health was zilch. I was covered in abscesses from head to toe, everywhere. I was only like 6 stone, nobody would talk to me, nobody liked me, I didn't like maself and I thought if I continued like this I'm going to die. So it came to the crunch when I decided to clean up, 'right Mary you're either goin' to die or you're goin' to clean up, what are you goin' to do?' And that's when I decided it's time to clean up.

(Mary)

Fourteen years of drug use had left Dorothy a 'broken' individual, 'mentally, physically and spiritually'.

> That's it in a nutshell. I couldn't take anymore, mentally, phys-
> ically and spiritually I was broke, I was wasted. I was killing
> maself, slowly committing suicide and I didn't even know it,
> d'you know what I mean? And I was goin' out and in places,
> hospitals and jails and institutions and all that stuff. My brain
> and my body were just so tired of it all. I'd had enough.
>
> *(Dorothy)*

Sometimes the recovering addicts would make no reference to identity, either directly or indirectly, when describing their rock bottom
experiences. For example, the crisis might be described purely in terms of
burn-out or physical deterioration and a fear of dying. However, the
omission of such references from their descriptions of the rock bottom
experience does not mean that identity was not a factor. Our interviewees did not account for their decision to quit and the circumstances
surrounding it in a neat and coherent fashion. Different aspects of the
process would be raised and explored in different parts of their narratives. It is therefore not surprising that aspects of the rock bottom experience may have been omitted from their description of it on the basis that
there was no point in repeating explanations emphasised elsewhere.
What is significant, however, is that, while it may not always have been
present in their descriptions of rock bottom, reference to the importance
of a desire to restore their identity invariably appeared elsewhere in their
accounts.

Although a rock bottom experience was a significant event for many of
our sample, the majority of them exited on the basis of what appeared
to be a rational choice. Consistent with Biernacki's work, this decision
usually followed prolonged exposure to a variety of negative, revealing
or shocking experiences which eventually forced addicts to review their
situation and to conclude that their addiction had to be broken in order
to repair an identity that had become seriously damaged and in order to
build a future that was in any sense acceptable to them. Our respondents
described these decisions in the following ways.

> Q I keep going back to this but what were you thinking when
> you realised this wasn't the kind of life you wanted? That
> you wanted to change it?

R   I don't know ... I was just sittin' thinking I don't want this life. Like you've got to pay like £35 to feel normal every day, it's no life. It's not the life I want, I don't want to go down those roads. Personally I think I'm too good for that, you know what I mean? Maself, I'm too good to go down those roads. I wanted to put a stop to it before it got any worse.

(Debbie)

I thought I am goin' to become a right low life or I am goin' to get better, one of those you know. You can pick or choose I was sayin' to myself you're going to have to pick because I knew, I was aware of what I was doing and I knew I didn't like it, not one little bit. Especially for someone that always had good clothes and that and always thought they were 'it'. Luckily I decided to get some help and I did.

(Douglas)

We are, however, somewhat uncomfortable with the use of the term 'rational decision' to describe this category since it implies a degree of consciousness which, according to our respondents, was not always present at the time their decision to give up drugs was taken. Our data suggest that, while some of the rational decision making was of the explicitly conscious variety described by Biernacki, much of it was not characterised by a conscious and studied balancing of the pros and cons of continuing to use drugs. Instead, our addicts' accounts suggest that the process is, for many, a much more unconscious one in which users gradually reach a point at which they simply come to *realise* that things have gone too far, that they have had enough, that drugs have inflicted too much damage on their lives and sense of self and that the time has come to stop.

Biernacki (1986) reports that two-thirds of his sample gave up drugs as a result of a rational decision while about one quarter to one third quit following a rock-bottom type crisis. The proportion of our sample who exited following a rock bottom experience was slightly higher than Biernacki's: 30 out of the 70 cases. However, Biernacki also identified a third method of giving up drugs which he refers to as 'drift'. This applies to people who 'without undergoing any especially traumatic experience and without forming a conscious, explicit resolve to change ... simply drift away from their addiction and get involved in other things' (1986,

p. 44). This category constituted a very small proportion of Biernacki's sample (about five per cent) and was not discernible among our addicts.

Both major exit routes involved the recognition of a spoiled identity and a resolution to put it right. For us, the main point of distinction between rational and rock bottom decisions is the difference between *wanting* and *having* to stop. The type of decision making that takes place is, in turn, a product of the extent to which the individual's identity is seen as having been damaged by their addiction. With rational decisions the individual decides that there are compelling reasons for wanting to stop, while with rock bottom decisions there is quite simply no sustainable alternative. In other words, the feature which distinguishes the rock bottom decision is a sense of having no choice. As a result, this type of decision tends to carry greater conviction and a higher level of motivation than a rational one. For those who reach rock bottom, it is a matter of giving up drugs or of being destroyed.

While, for most addicts, a decision of some sort, based on a desire to restore one's identity, appeared to be a necessary prelude to a successful exit from drug use, neither type of decision – rational or rock bottom – was sufficient to guarantee that success. Although a substantial proportion of the addicts in our sample exited finally on the basis of a rational choice, not all succeeded at their first attempt. Certainly, a number of our respondents reported having relapsed following attempts to stop based on rational decisions. In addition, most of those who reach rock bottom have usually passed through the stage of wanting and trying to stop on the basis of a rational decision-making process. Indeed, usually rock bottom comes at the end of a sequence of failed attempts and could be seen almost as a last resort for those who fail to get out of drugs by other means. Although we encountered no examples of a rock bottom experience that was followed by relapse, it would be surprising if this did not occur in some cases since, given the power of drug addiction, no decision to stop can be an absolute guarantee of success. It is possible that those who failed to quit following a rock bottom decision did not appear in our sampling frame because they had entered some personal abyss which precluded successful contact with them. Others, of course, may have exited through suicide.

As we saw, it is certainly not necessary to hit rock bottom in order to quit drugs successfully. On the other hand, of course, neither is a rock bottom decision a guarantee of success. What our research does suggest, however, is that the likelihood of success may be considerably higher with a rock bottom decision because the motivation is that much greater.

Ambivalence

A striking feature of the period surrounding a rational decision to stop and the attempt that is based on it, is that it is frequently characterised by a great deal of ambivalence on the part of the addict. What happens is that the addict experiences conflict between a desire to change on the one hand and a reluctance to give up the drug on the other. Part of them wants to stop because they believe it to be the right thing to do for the sake of their future and their self-respect. At the same time, though, they fear the pain and discomfort of withdrawal and, in addition, sometimes continue to derive pleasure from the drug itself.

It is clear from the literature on drug addiction that this sort of ambivalence is endemic to the lives of addicts and that it is present for a large part of their drug-using career (Prins 1994, Biernacki 1986). For example, Stimson and Oppenheimer report that 'nearly every addict said at some time that he or she wanted to stop and yet at the same time wanted to continue using drugs' (1982, p. 157). Shaffer (1992) has portrayed the roots of the addict's dilemma very graphically and concisely in the statement, 'addictive behaviours serve while they destroy' (p. 101). One of our respondents, Judy, described her ambivalence in the following way, eventually admitting that the problem was that she did not really want to stop using drugs.

> I was wantin' to come off but I had no will power know what I mean, I had no will power at all. Drugs were too big an addiction for me. I wanted them so obviously ma heart wasn't in it. I didn't really want to come off that much.
>
> *(Judy)*

The main reason for addicts' reluctance to stop despite wanting to do so is the continuing allure of the drug combined with their physiological dependence on it. In the view of our interviewees, unless and until the pleasurable effects of the drug disappear, stopping is, at best, extremely difficult.

> At the time it was like part of me was wantin' to try it [coming off] and a big part of me wasn't, was still wantin' me to keep on using. 'Cos they'd been ma life for so long, they had been a big part of ma life for so long. And it was goin' to be a big loss d'you know what I mean.
>
> *(Dorothy)*

However, even when the drug no longer confers any pleasure, there is still the hurdle of physical dependence to negotiate and, for all addicts, the prospect of facing the pain and distress of withdrawal is a daunting one. They will frequently have experienced withdrawal personally – either voluntarily or involuntarily – and, in addition, will often have observed its harsh effects on others. What this means is that a desire to give up drugs, however strong, can be frustrated for lengthy periods, even indefinitely, by an understandable reluctance to face the rigours of withdrawal.

> Although I really wanted to be clean, I didn't as well, it was like a pull, a two-way thing. There was a bit of me really wantin' to be clean and just the easy option was to keep using.
>
> *(Angela)*

As a consequence of this, some addicts' careers skip attempts to exit based on a rational decision and they only come off when they hit rock bottom.

Maturing out of addiction

We believe our study may help to enhance our understanding of the process by which many addicts appear to 'mature out' of their addiction sometime in their thirties. We would suggest that this process is likely to be closely related to the recognition of a spoiled identity and to the temporality of the factors which promote this recognition and encourage and facilitate the decision to change. In short, we believe that there are naturally occurring tendencies in the careers of addicts which, over time, increasingly predispose or channel them towards a decision to stop. Our study suggests that there may be two main elements in this process. First, it is likely to be associated with certain aspects of the social career of the drug taker. In particular, in common with non-users, addicts over time increasingly develop close relationships with others and acquire a sense of responsibility for and towards them. Prominent among these significant others are partners and children. As we saw earlier, their relationships with those individuals play a prominent part in gradually revealing the nature and extent of the addict's spoiled identity and in re-awakening his or her interest in the future. In other words, these developing relationships and their associated responsibilities are one of the primary mechanisms through which the addict recognises the need to change. Second, 'maturing out' may also be partly a product of the natural history of drug-taking and of the changing effect of the drug itself. As we noted earlier, a significant feature of the experience of addiction is that, in time, the drug loses its ability to confer pleasure and, increasingly, maintaining the habit comes to be seen by the addict as being problematic and burdensome. As a consequence of this, the longer the addict's career lasts, the less it is likely to be determined by the pharmacology of the drug and the more other factors will be able to exert their influence. We argued earlier that this alteration in the role and effect of the drug is likely to be a necessary condition for successful exit from drug misuse.

Traditionally, the term 'maturing out' has been applied solely to the process by which some addicts give up drugs 'naturally'; in other words, without the assistance of treatment (Winick 1962, Biernacki 1986, Prins 1994). However, we believe that this may represent too narrow a view of the processes involved. Specifically, we suggest that it is possible to regard the 'maturing' process which we have described as applying just as much to those addicts who overcome their addiction with the assistance of treatment. What is common, and crucial, to both routes out is the decision to stop using. It is this decision that is the most significant step for addicts on the road to recovery and, once it has been made, whether the route out is via treatment agencies or not is of secondary importance. We would argue that this decision is heavily influenced, for both routes out, by the nature of the addict's evolving social attachments and the changing pharmacology of the drug.

Conclusion

In this chapter, we have argued that the key element in a successful attempt to give up illegal drugs is a desire on the part of the addict to restore an identity, which has been badly damaged by his or her drug-using lifestyle. This is not, of course, to say that other factors and considerations were not also important in the decision to quit. Clearly, they were. However, our research suggests that their main significance lay in their ability to reveal to the addicts how low they had sunk and to engender in them a desire to rebuild their shattered identities and lives. According to the recovering addicts in our study, giving up drugs for reasons that were not to do with changing their identities might work for a time but, in the great majority of cases, eventually led to relapse.

In the next chapter we show how some addicts' awareness of how their drug use was having a negative impact on one particular set of relationships was an important part of the process of coming off drugs.

4 Parenting, children and recovery

In this chapter we look at the impact which the addicts' drug use had on their children and, in particular, at the way in which their growing awareness of that impact played an important part in their recovery. Although not all of the individuals interviewed in our research were parents, 30 of the 70 recovering addicts whom we interviewed spoke at length, and usually without prompting, about the way in which their drug use had affected their children and about how this realisation had influenced their decision to give up drugs. Before looking in detail at what our recovering addicts had to say about their children, we would like to discuss briefly why children appear to have played such a prominent part in the recovery of so many of them.

In some respects the state of being a drug addict can be characterised as one of extreme self-centredness. For the addict, his or her world is effectively reduced to two elements: the addict him or herself and the drugs that he or she is using. Everything else it seems – family, friends, hobbies, occupation and so on – fades into insignificance in comparison. The essential self-centredness of the addict state is well illustrated in the extract below. In this passage, Sharon, one of the addict parents, returns home to find that her house has been ransacked by a knife-wielding gang looking for her son. As she reveals, while she is clearly concerned for her son's welfare, she is even more worried that the gang might have discovered the drugs that she had hidden in the house. In other words, her next 'hit' was of greater importance to her than her son's welfare. She confesses, 'You're not really that bothered about what's happened to him. To be really honest, you're just worrying about what you're going to do for your hit.'

There was a big rammy in the street and they were running around and Gerry [son] was getting chased round the streets with these guys with swords in broad daylight. And seemingly there was a gang of them and they came charging into the house. I don't know how he got out but I think if they had actually got him they would have run him through. I came in another night and I knew the house had been turned over and I couldn't find him. And I thought, 'oh my God', and you're trying to find him and at the same time you know there was something in the house and you're thinking oh no but he was all right they had not found him. But at the same time you're thinking I hope they haven't found the drugs because you're going to be left with nothing if they found them. You're not really that bothered about what's happened to him. To be really honest, you're just worrying about what you're going to do for your hit. You become quite self-centred and selfish as well, you're just thinking about yourself.

(Sharon)

Given the self-centred nature of the addict's world, it is perhaps not surprising that so many of the individuals interviewed in our research emphasised the importance of coming off drugs for oneself. It was no good attempting to come off for other people, no matter how negative the effects of the addict's habit upon them. The recovery from drug addiction was simply too big a challenge to be achieved for other people and, from the depths of their addiction, other people had ceased to be that important to them anyway.

While the state of being a drug addict can be characterised as being one of extreme self-centredness, the process of recovery can be seen, in part at least, as being about a growing awareness of other people and of the way in which the individual's drug use has had an impact upon them. As we saw earlier, other people were central to the addict's recovery, not because they provided the motivation for it but rather because they reflected back to the addict the person he or she had become as a result of drug use. It was in this sense that other people could act as a catalyst to the addict's recovery. However, it was evident from our research that not all relationships with other people were equally powerful in providing the addict with a reflection of the person he or she had become as a result of drug use.

While many of our recovering addicts had friends and family members whose lives had been adversely affected by their addiction, it did not appear from the addicts' accounts that these relationships were as salient in their recovery as their relationships with their children. The reason for this may have had to do with the fact that the addict's relationships with other people were an imperfect reflection of the addict's own life. It was always possible for the addict to interpret these relationships in terms of those individuals' own lives and actions rather than as being, even in part, a consequence of the addict's behaviour. The situation in relation to the addict's own children was very different in this respect. What was different about the addict's children was that the content and quality of their lives were very largely dependent upon the addict. Given this dependence, the lives of his or her children could be seen as representing a perfect mirror image of the person the addict had become as a result of his or her drug use. In recounting how their drug use had impacted upon their children our interviewees were not so much saying 'my child has had an awful life', but rather, 'my child has been exposed to things that they should never have been exposed to, has seen things that they should never have seen, and done things they should never have done, because of the person I became as a result of my drug use'. From the addicts' own perspective, the lives of their children were the perfect illustration of their most profound failure.

The impact of parental drug use on children

Many of the addict parents spoke at length about how their drug use had disrupted their children's world. Part of that disruption had to do with the marked mood swings they would experience, depending upon whether they were enjoying the effects of recent drug use, or facing the unpleasant effects of drug withdrawal.

> When I was on drugs, if I was to go two days without it, I'd take it out on my kids. I would turn around and say 'it's your fault I've not got drugs'. If they moaned for the least wee thing I'd jump down their throat. I'd not hit them but I knew in my own mind I shouldn't have been doing that. It wasn't their fault I was on drugs so why should I let them suffer.
>
> *(Brenda)*

> When I was using, I was happy with my kids and that but it was a false happiness, I know that. It's a false caring for them 'cos when

I'd come down off the speed I tended to get edgy with them, kind of touchy. And then when I was happy they knew the difference but they didn't understand it, if you know what I mean. To me that's terrible for me as a mother.

(Maggie)

It is clear from these accounts, that for these two women their relationship with their children, during the period of their drug use, was fundamentally at odds with their notion of how a mother should behave towards them. It was obviously deeply upsetting for them to acknowledge how far short their own parenting fell from their idea of how a mother ought to be.

A further element of disruption to the children's world arose as a result of the many periods in their lives when they had to be cared for by other adults as a result of their own parents' inability to look after them. Their children's experiences of being separated from them and being cared for by others could have a profound effect upon their mother or father as Paula reveals in the following extract.

And it was torture when I was going to visit ma children. When they saw me I think they thought they were coming home 'cos they would say, oh you're back mammy. And I was like 'oh son now you can't come home now'. And what made it worse was the two of them were split up when they were in care. The oldest one was with one family and the wee one was with another family so they weren't even together. And when you were going away after the visiting they would be screaming and clinging onto you and the social workers would be dragging them away and I thought, fuck I can't handle this, I can't go through this, watching them doing this now. It was really cutting me up inside.

(Paula)

In addition, the frequent involvement of other people in caring for their children could undermine the addict's relationship with them in a range of other more subtle ways. In particular, parents could come to feel excluded from their child's development and achievements.

Well you see he was in foster care for all bar 11 months. I've got him three days a week having to watch him going away and leaving and screaming. Then you see him coming on and you're not responsible for him, it's not you that taught him how to talk and it's not you that potty trained him and things like that. Things like that catch up with you.

(Marion)

Another negative impact on the child's social world was associated with the fact that they frequently had to accompany their parents on their never-ending search for drugs. What made this especially disruptive for the child was the fact that these outings often occurred late at night or in the early hours of the morning. Judy viewed the fact that she had subjected her child to such rigours with an obvious sense of revulsion.

I'd seen the likes of people going for drugs with their kids in their pram sort of thing and it just used to make me feel sick to the pit of my stomach, know what I mean. Even though it had to be done, there was no way I'd put her through that again.

(Judy)

However, it was not just the quest for drugs that was witnessed by children. Many of them also observed their parents' drug-taking directly. Mark and Sharon were typical in reporting that, while they were using drugs, they did not particularly care what their children saw. Their priority was their drug-taking, not their children's welfare.

I always said I would never jag in front of him, everybody always says that but see if it came to it and he walked into the toilet when I was putting that in ma arm I wouldn't pull it out. He'd see things like jellies and that all lying about and things like that.

(Sharon)

I still can't put it into words to this day how I feel about it, and the fact that he's seen a lot of things he shouldn't have seen when he was growing up. He was parked in the room when people wanted to inject. If he didn't stay in the room he'd maybe walk in and we'd be sitting with a needle in our arm. He's seen a lot of things he shouldn't have seen and that's what I feel guilty about.

(Mark)

In addition to the guilt which many addict parents felt about what their children had been exposed to, some also expressed profound regret at what they saw as their failure to protect their children from certain risks. For example, Kathleen believed that being under the influence of drugs had prevented her from protecting her child from being abused by her partner.

> My eldest son had bruises on the side of his face and I think it was my partner that had hit him, but I was too out of my face to notice. I just hold on to things like that, what could have happened and in fact what has happened.
>
> *(Kathleen)*

Kathleen also indicates that her partial awareness of what might have happened, and of how much worse things could have been without her knowing about it or being able to intervene to protect her child, was something that she held on to as an important element in her recovery: 'I just hold on to things like that, what could have happened and in fact what has happened.' Episodes such as these stood as a vivid testimony to the parents' inability to protect their children and were experienced by the individuals concerned as the ultimate personal failure.

Many of the addict parents spoke about the choices they had made in prioritising their drug use in preference to the welfare of their children. One of the most obvious ways in which such prioritisation occurred was in relation to money. The extent to which her children had been deprived as a consequence of her drug use was brought home to Pauline in a poignant way by her eldest son's reaction to receiving a small amount of money.

> The more people told me I had a problem the more I would deny I had a problem. And it was one night when I'd sold all the furniture in the house and the children were really starving and instead of running about trying to get them food I was running about trying to get my drugs. In the end I think the shame caught up with me, and the guilt. Stevie, my eldest son, had been given a pound by somebody and he was hanging on to this pound note like it was gold and it just all of a sudden brought me to my senses. What the fuck have I been doing to these children? It was this pound note, he was making so much of it that it was like gold to him and this was the biggest thing that had happened to Stevie in his life for a long, long time.
>
> *(Pauline)*

However, the neglect of their children's needs in preference to their own needs as addicts was not just about money or their ability to provide for their children in a material way. As Frances records, the neglect applied to every aspect of their children's lives.

> I really neglected the kids because o' my drugs. They weren't properly fed and their clothes, just generally neglected. And I didn't bother with what they were doing, who they were going about with, how they were getting on at school or anything. It was just drugs, drugs, drugs.
>
> *(Frances)*

According to some of the addict parents, their children had to take on quasi-parental responsibilities, such as caring for younger siblings, as a way of compensating for their parent's shortcomings in this respect.

> I think the fact that I had ma wee boy about me helped me. At the same time I knew I was destroying his life. I felt helpless, but there was still a part of me that wanted to be responsible for him and stuff like that. He was doing everything for himself, just like grown up at four years old, so grown up, it just made me feel, 'oh he's OK he doesn't need me', and that you know . . . It got to the stage when he was having to look after his wee brother, he was sort of having to play mummy and daddy you know, he'd get up in the morning and make his bottle because mummy and daddy are lying on the bed sparked from the night before. So it really affected my oldest boy.
>
> *(Jane)*

Conscious that their children's needs were suffering as a result of their need for drugs, a number of the parents reported embarking on sprees of lavish gift-giving as a way of compensating and atoning for what they saw as their neglect. Once given, however, such presents could subsequently be seen as a way of generating the necessary income with which to buy drugs.

> When my daughter was born people were giving her presents, clothes and that. When I started dabbling again though, I started selling her clothes. I started to forget about the child. You buy them new clothes and, when you are full of it, you sell them.

Giving it with one hand and taking it away with the other. The child wasn't getting any love. I don't care what anybody says, when you're taking drugs you're trying to buy their love off them. Give them clothes, give them this and that, the best of gear. There's no loving, there's no true feeling or anything like that.

(Brenda)

Some of the addict parents also commented that, as a result of their drug use, their children's knowledge of drugs was much more detailed than that of their peers. This could often be a source of embarrassment and anxiety for them. For example, Judy and her children had moved from inner-city Edinburgh to a small village on the outskirts of the city to get away from drugs. However, this had brought her, and her children, into contact with new friends and neighbours and this, in turn, had made her realise how different her own children's upbringing had been compared to that of their new neighbours' children.

It's better for the kids here as well. They're out playing in big fields and doing things like fishing and things that they would never have done . . . There was a few kids in the house the other day and Colin my wee boy used to smoke hash and one of the wee lassies, she's nearly twelve, she turned round and said what's that? And Colin looked at her as if to say, 'everybody should know that' sort of thing. Saturday, we were having this discussion at the table and he didn't realise that hash was a drug, he thought that was normal. It just shows you. I think in nearly every house they used to go into when they lived in Edinburgh there would be people sticking cigarette papers together and things but you don't realise they're like that, you don't think you're doing that to them, which is quite bad.

(Judy)

Many of the children of addict parents had also been exposed to petty or more serious forms of criminal behaviour associated with their parents' drug use. Fiona's description of her son's experience of her criminal activities is a good example of this.

My oldest boy was treble streetwise 'cos he was brought up that way. He'd been in the jail and things like that with us [visiting relatives] and I'd take him out [stealing] with me, get the jail and my mum would need to come down to the police station and get him and things like that.

(Fiona)

As some of the parents explained, exposing their children to such criminal behaviour at an early age could result in their children accepting the criminal lifestyle as being perfectly normal. In the extract below, Lorna describes how she became aware of this happening with her own son when she took him to buy his first pair of shoes.

I remember my oldest boy when I bought him his first pair of shoes, he wanted a pair of Chelsea boots and I thought I'm going to get him them and I went in and bought him them. I was so excited I phoned my sister, 'I've bought the child a pair of boots'. And she was like 'Lorna you're meant to do that' and I said 'yea I know but I'm not used to going in'. See the day I was in buying him them boots, that's when I seen what I was doing to him. It's all right laughing about it now, it's quite funny when you think about it 'cos he's got the boots on and he's looking at me and he's kicked his old ones under the seat. I'm watching him do this and I'm like 'we don't do that anymore, just take the boots off'. He took the boots off, and I've gone to pay for them and it wasn't till we came out of the shop and I've looked at him and I've thought 'God love you', 'cos that was the kind of thing I'd done with him before. I'd be like come on and be pushing him out of the door and things like that. And I was sort of trying to explain to him 'look son, we don't do that now, we pay for things now', and he was looking at me 'alright'. He was starting to go into shops stealing and things like that. He was caught a couple of times in shops along [name of street] stealing and it was just because he thought that was the way you done it, it was a way of life.

(Lorna)

In recounting the various ways in which their drug use had affected their children, many of these addicts were articulating what they saw as their failure as parents. The many adverse experiences which their children had faced were, by the addicts' own admission, their responsibility. It was they, the addicts, who had determined these experiences and it was in this sense that their children represented the clearest example of their failure.

So far in this chapter we have looked at the various ways in which the parents' drug use was seen by them as having had a negative impact on their children. We now turn to look at the ways in which the children themselves appear to have had an impact on their parents' drug use.

The impact of children on their parents' drug use

So powerful were the addicts' feelings about the possible impact of their drug-using lifestyle on their children that for some individuals even the knowledge that they were going to have children was sufficient to make them reassess their drug use.

> Yea well we actually asked for a detox unit for the two of us to see if we can do it together. 'Cos she's pregnant again and I just got the jail for shoplifting. When I'm in the jail she just struggles and when she struggles the child suffers and if the child suffers I suffer. So I've got to get off.
>
> *(Glen)*

For some of the expectant mothers, it was the effect that their drug-taking might have on the health of their unborn child that was their greatest concern.

> These were the main concerns for me. I didn't want to have a junkie baby and I didn't want to pump ma system full of that crap when I was pregnant that would affect the baby.
>
> *(Chrissy)*

Given the multiplicity of ways in which their drug-taking could have a negative impact on their children, it is perhaps not surprising that many of the addict parents sought to conceal their drug use from them. In particular, they would often try to keep the business of acquiring and actually taking the drug secret from their children. However, according to the parents, their attempts to achieve this became less and less effective as the children themselves became increasingly aware of their surroundings and could see through what was happening.

> I need off because the children are getting older and I'm 27. I see people now, I mean they're in their late thirties and you look at

them and I don't want to be like that at that age. I think it's bad enough being on them now at 27, I know people near enough 40 and that's not a good thing. Their children are 12 and 13. I don't want mine seeing that. I don't want my children seeing me like that at that age . . .

(Kenny)

In addition to parents' anxiety that their children would become aware of their drug use, there was an even greater fear that their example might encourage their children to follow in their footsteps and start to use drugs themselves. This, for many of the addict parents, was the greatest fear of all. They did not want their children's lives to be destroyed in the same way as their own had been.

I didn't want the kids following in my footsteps, I knew the lifestyle I was leading, that was what they were seeing, that was what they thought was acceptable, and that was the lifestyle they would grow into, and I was scared for them, really scared for them.

(Ian)

The risk that children might follow their parents into drugs was compounded by the fact that not only did the parents believe they were providing an inappropriate role model, their ability to dissuade them from experimenting with drugs was also seriously compromised. As Claire indicates, any attempt to persuade children not to follow their parents' example would simply be seen as hypocrisy.

I mean do you think for one minute I ever wanted them to know I'd been on this. What chance have they got, how could I tell them not to do something when I'm doing it. You're just a hypocrite and I'm no' prepared to do that. I wouldn't even smoke hash in front of the kids. As far as they are concerned drugs are bad things and I'll keep to that.

(Claire)

Another important aspect of children's role as witnesses to the negative impact of their parent's addiction is the way in which the children's advancing years provided an unequivocal measure of the passage of time. First of all, with each passing year these children were a powerful reminder of just how long their parents had been locked into their addiction:

> My wee lassie is eight, I was at her birthday and that really stunned me, she's eight now, where have the years gone. Know what I mean, it's like when I look at my son, do I wait till he's eight and she's sixteen and go. No I'd better go into a rehab now, know what I mean.
>
> *(Patrick)*

In addition, though, the increasing age of their children could also provoke a powerful sense of time running out and of the loss of opportunities to do things with their children that would never reappear:

> I want to be able to give my children things like I used to not be able to do. I want to take them places, I want to do things with them.
>
> *(Douglas)*

It is evident from what we have said so far that many of the addict parents felt incredibly guilty about the many ways in which their drug use had affected the lives of their children. The nature of their failure as parents that this represented was, for many of our interviewees, a powerful catalyst for them to attempt to give up drugs. It was also evident from our interviews that many of the addict parents sought to measure the success of their recovery in terms of how successful they had been in rebuilding their relationships with their children. In this sense, the children of addict parents had an impact on their parents' drug use that went far beyond the desire to come off drugs.

> As I said, I've got two bairns. They'll stop me from using and I won't use again. I like just getting up in the morning and being straight. That's three-and-a-half years down the road and I still enjoy being straight. It was the first buzz I ever got when I came off it. Just getting up in the morning and not needing a hit. I'm still like that, still get up in the morning, not every morning, but some mornings I get up and go 'fuck, I don't need anything this morning'. My kids can come in today and say, 'all right dad?' And one time they couldn't, because I was erratic. If they came in my room I'd be like, 'Get to fuck'. My kids were afraid of me and

now they love me you know. And that's a good feeling again.
Even the feeling of going out to my mum and dad's and they love
us, they love us being round about them 'cos three years ago they
didn't want anything to do with me. Today I'm back to my best,
I'm probably better than ever.

(Colin)

It is interesting in this extract from Colin's interview that the two sets
of relationships which are cited as evidence of his recovery are those with
his parents and his children. As we have just indicated, a number of our
interviewees spontaneously referred to their improved relationships with
their children as an important measure of their changed lives. Often it
was the most basic and, in other circumstances, trivial aspects of
parenting that provided them with a real sense of pleasure.

Q   What can you do now that you couldn't do before?

R   Get up in the morning smiling, joke, carry on with the kids,
have a laugh, just being a mother. As much as I thought and
believed I was a mother before, I wasn't, do you know what
I mean? It's myself I was thinking about all of the time. And
like I can do things and feel good about it. I'll come in and
I mean, I was hopeless at cooking, I never cooked anything.
I came in and made beefburgers and I was all proud of
myself. And these small things give you a buzz. Everyday
things. It's good you get a good feeling . . . The other day I
got a phone call from the school about my son and I felt
great that I could actually run up there with no drugs in me
and, do you know what I mean, be there for him. 'Cos it
wasn't me that was there before for them, it was a maniac.
It makes me feel good to see the difference in them too,
smiling and glad to see me back. It was getting to the stage
they just didn't want to be with me. Now that's all changed
and if they run in from school I can hear them shouting
'where's my mum' and that makes you smile, it's good to
hear all that.

(Lesley)

For some addicts the fact of having to care for their children was of
great assistance in the process of coming off drugs. Apart from anything

else, the requirements involved in looking after a child provided an opportunity to become involved in meaningful non-drug-related activities.

> I've got a family this time. In the past I didn't have my kids there to keep me off it, but now I've got one kid and another on the way so this time that'll be me off for good.
>
> *(Tina)*

So powerful was the incentive which children provided to stay off drugs, that one of our interviewees even claimed that having children was a conscious part of her strategy for remaining drug-free.

> I think the kids keep me going. I think that's why I've got so many you know. To keep off drugs I just need to keep having children. People go, 'Oh God, how do you cope with all these kids?' I like staying in and playing daft games, doing stupid things. Maybe I'm just a big kid myself. I probably manage better with five than some people with one or two ... I think that keeps me going. There are weeks when maybe the only people I see are the people in here.
>
> *(Joyce)*

At first sight it might seem rather strange to describe having children as part of a strategy for staying off drugs. However, one can see clearly in the extract above how the heavy demands of parenting multiple children could fill an individual's time and assist in breaking drug-using relationships. As we show in the next chapter, being able to fill the empty hours left behind once drugs are no longer the sole focus of the addict's life is an essential element in recovery.

So far in this chapter we have discussed parents' awareness of the impact of their drug use on their children and vice versa. However, our interviewees also revealed that the process of coming off drugs could itself give rise to a further set of unanticipated problems with their children. For example, some parents were anxious about how, when and whether to tell their children about their past drug use and about the things that had happened to the children at that time.

> When I was through all this and off [drugs] I still had a lot of trouble with the children trying to settle them down and things like that. The oldest would always try and kind of emotionally

blackmail me. Say that he wished he was back in care and things like that when he couldn't get what he wanted and that. And it was sore, really sore, when I saw what it had done. Especially the oldest one, he could remember more about me using than I could because he'd seen it all. The fact that he was put in foster care because I didn't want him, I had to sit down and try to explain to him: 'Look son this was the score and you need to try and understand the way it was.'

(Helen)

Some parents, on the other hand, derived considerable comfort from the fact that their children appeared not to remember much about their past drug use:

They don't seem to remember, we've been having conversations about things like that [drugs] and if they're watching films or that they'll say 'And did you do that and do you know anybody that does that?' and things like that.

(Graham)

As we have seen, then, the children of addict parents were important elements in their parents' recovery in two ways. First, they prompted a recognition of how far they had sunk by mirroring the way in which their addict lifestyle had affected their children. Second, they played an important part in helping to maintain the addicts' resolve during the recovery process.

Conclusion

In an editorial in the journal *Addiction*, Marina Barnard (1999) has called for greater attention to be focused upon the needs of addict parents and their children. This is important not least because of the growing numbers of children living within family homes where one or both parents are dependent upon illegal drugs. In Glasgow, with a population of around 650,000, it has been estimated that there may be between 7000 and 10,000 children living within such households while the figure for the UK as a whole could be as high as 280,000. In the light of these numbers there is a pressing need to assess the situation of children and parents in addict households. On the basis of the views of the recovering addicts in our study, there can be little doubt that drug addiction can undermine parents' ability to care for their children. For the majority of addict parents interviewed in our research, there was a fundamental conflict between the demands of looking after one's children and the pursuit of a drug-using lifestyle. As we have attempted to show in this chapter, the parents' growing awareness of how their drug use had affected their children was a tremendously powerful catalyst for their recovery. The image of themselves, which they saw reflected back in the lives of their children, was one of ultimate failure. In their own eyes they had failed to meet the most basic of human responsibilities; namely, the care of their own children. In that failure the addicts came to see that they had become the people they least wanted to be. However, we also saw that the addicts' recovery from dependent drug use could be measured in terms of their relationships with their children. To the extent that they had been able to rebuild those relationships, our interviewees were able to gauge how far they had moved from being the people they were in the midst of their addiction.

Children were, then, central to the eventual recovery of many of our addicts. Our finding in this regard mirrors closely that of Graham and Bowling (1995) who, in their research on young people and crime, noted that having children was one of the strongest predictors for individuals ceasing to offend.

> All of the mothers interviewed spoke of the profoundly positive influence that children had on their lives, outlook, identity, sense of responsibility and behaviour. Several young women stated that responsibility for children had brought about a complete change in their lifestyle, they drank less, used fewer drugs, socialised less, saw their friends less and stopped offending. (Graham and Bowling 1995, p. 73)

While the positive effects of having children were most dramatically evident among female offenders in Graham and Bowling's study, there were indications of a similar effect among many of the male offenders as well. The authors of this study offer an explanation for their findings on the role of children by suggesting that 'the sense of responsibility engendered by parenthood . . . leads to changes in the way in which the needs of other people are perceived which, in turn, are linked to cognitive changes which reduce propensities to commit offences. Having children forces one to think of the consequences of one's own actions, including criminal actions' (1995, p. 76).

In our own research, children were important in the eventual recovery of many of our addicts because they provided such an uncompromising image of the person the addict had become as a result of his or her drug use. It is possible that other dependent relationships, for example with elderly parents, could provide a similar, though perhaps less extreme form of influence. We say less extreme because, within our society, the normative importance attached to looking after one's elderly parents is somewhat less than that associated with looking after one's children. Nevertheless, where the addict has elderly parents or other dependants, it is possible that the addict's failure to care for these individuals may also be experienced as a profound personal failure and thereby function as a similar catalyst to the individual's recovery.

In the final chapter of this book we consider the implications of our findings for drug services generally. However, we would like to note one implication, which arises from the analysis we have presented in this chapter. If it is the case, as we have sought to show, that children are often an important element in their parents' recovery then it suggests that drug-treatment services ought perhaps to give greater weight than they do at present to the role of children in this process. In particular, there may be merit in services addressing with addicts the way in which their drug use is affecting their children. It is unlikely that such an approach is going to result in a sudden conversion on the part of the individuals concerned. However, over time, addicts may come to an awareness of the way in which their drug use has affected their children and the self-knowledge derived from that understanding might well assist individuals in their eventual recovery.

In the next chapter, we look in detail at what the recovering addicts had to say about the process of staying off drugs.

5 Staying off

A common feature of the biography of most drug addicts is that their careers are likely to be peppered with numerous attempts to escape from their addiction. Periods of abstinence can last from a few days to a few years but, by definition, the great majority of these end in failure. A number of estimates suggest that rates of relapse among treated populations can be as high as 90 per cent (Smart 1994, Christo 1998). Clearly, then, the key to successful recovery from drug addiction lies not simply in the addict's ability to stop taking drugs; of at least equal importance is his or her ability to stay off. Accordingly, a crucial question, which has to be addressed, is: what are the factors and circumstances which assist or impede recovering addicts in their attempts to maintain abstinence and avoid becoming re-addicted?

Most of the research on this topic has concentrated on exploring the reasons for relapse following treatment or spontaneous periods of abstinence. According to this work, factors which are of particular significance in precipitating relapse are: the addict's craving or continuing desire for the drug (Simpson et al. 1986, McAuliffe et al. 1986, Heather and Stallard 1989, Gossop et al. 1991); negative emotional states such as depression, loneliness or boredom (Cummings et al. 1980, Rhoads 1983, Judson and Goldstein 1983, Marlatt and Gordon 1985, Bradley et al. 1989, Hall et al. 1991); the experience of stressful or conflictual situations (Cummings et al. 1980, Kosten et al. 1986) and pressure from others to resume drug use (Cummings et al. 1980, Marlatt and Gordon 1985, Myres and Brown 1990).

However, these risks, or predisposing factors, do not lead inevitably to relapse. Many addicts recover successfully in spite of these negative experiences (see Biernacki 1986). What this means is that information on the factors associated with relapse provides only part of the answer to the question of how and why some addicts are able to sustain their recovery and remain drug-free while others are not. While a considerable amount of research has been devoted to predicting the occurrence of relapse, much less work has been conducted on the factors and circumstances which may help to prevent it, including the ways in which former addicts may seek to protect themselves from becoming re-addicted (Christo 1998). More specifically, relatively little research has been carried out on the strategies which recovering addicts employ in order to maintain abstinence or on how these strategies relate to each other.

The limited number of sociological studies that have been carried out in this area suggest that the key to successful recovery from addiction is the construction, by the addict, of a new identity incorporating non-addict values and perspectives and a non-addict lifestyle. For example, on the basis of his study of recovery from opiate addiction, Biernacki (1986) argues that 'To change their lives successfully, addicts must fashion new identities, perspectives and social world involvements wherein the addict identity is excluded or dramatically depreciated' (p. 141). Essential to the success of this process is the acceptance of the addict into the social worlds of non-addiction. Biernacki (1986) and Waldorf (1983) have between them described the strategies used, both by treated and untreated former opiate addicts, to support the development of new identities and maintain their abstinence from drugs. These include: moving away from the drug scene and their former drug-using associates; developing a new drug-free lifestyle; making sure that they occupy their time as fully as possible and in ways that do not pose a threat to their new status; and the use of other drugs – usually alcohol or marijuana – as a substitute for the one they have given up. Both agree that finding employment, preferably of a paid variety, and the support of family and friends can make a major contribution to this process. The importance of avoiding drug-using friends is reinforced by a number of other studies (e.g. Cummings et al. 1980, Stimson and Oppenheimer 1982, Simpson et al. 1986, Gossop et al. 1989). Similarly, several studies have confirmed the significance of social support in helping former drug addicts or alcoholics to remain abstinent (Rhoads 1983, Judson and Goldstein 1983, Gossop et al. 1989, Sobell et al. 1991, Klingemann 1992). Biernacki (1986) and Waldorf (1983) argue that, in time, the former addict's new life and identity come to act as an effective barrier against returning to a life on drugs. As Waldorf puts it, the ex-addicts come to fear the loss of what they have achieved and '. . . become locked into a life which has little place for opiate use' (p. 269).

Stall and Biernacki (1986) have broadened this analysis to include forms of addiction other than heroin abuse. Applying an interactionist perspective to a review of studies of spontaneous remission from the problematic use of alcohol, food/obesity, tobacco and opiates, they identify four processes, which they claim are especially significant as far as sustained recovery is concerned. The first of these is the creation of a new, non-using identity and its negotiation and acceptance by significant others in the straight world. This they regard as being the key element in the process of recovery. Second, it is vital that the former addict integrates into non-drug-using networks, partly because it helps to keep the ex-user away from temptation and partly because these networks provide the means of validating his or her new identity. Third, support from others plays an important part in helping to maintain the former users' resolve to persevere in overcoming their addiction. Finally, 'positive feedback' in the form of improved social, economic and emotional status also makes a significant contribution to the recovery process by making the ex-user's efforts appear worthwhile.

In this chapter we look at the strategies, which the recovering addicts in our study used to maintain their abstinence from illegal drugs (see also McIntosh and McKeganey 2000a). Our concern here is with the processes and factors which appear to promote sustained and lasting recovery from addiction.

Restoring a spoiled identity

In Chapter 3, we argued that successful attempts to give up drugs are usually motivated by the desire on the part of addicts to restore an identity that has been badly spoiled by their addiction and by their immersion in the world of drugs. A decision to quit which was based on an attempt by the addict to recapture a positive sense of self appeared to stand a much better chance of success than one which was motivated by a desire to achieve some practical objective such as holding on to one's children or persuading an erstwhile partner to return. According to our interviewees, the latter type of decision usually led to relapse and it was only when they were motivated by a resolve to repair a damaged identity and regain their self-respect that their attempt to abstain was likely to succeed. In this chapter we do two things. Firstly, we examine the means – the mechanisms and strategies – through which the recovering addicts whom we interviewed sought to effect this transformation in their identities. Secondly, we explore the factors and circumstances which encouraged, impeded or sustained them in their efforts to achieve this.

The restoration of a spoiled identity cannot be achieved by the simple act of the addict declaring that he or she has stopped taking drugs; a renewed sense of self has to be built and constantly defended against a variety of often-powerful opposing forces. Just as the addict's reason for quitting is to recapture a positive sense of self, the task for the recovering addict is to construct and sustain this new identity. As we will see, this is not an easy task. The transformation from addict to non-addict involves profound changes in the individuals' lives – particularly in their daily activities and relationships – and most of these changes have to be managed actively by the addicts themselves. In other words, they have to work very hard at the transition.

One of the reasons why the transition is so difficult is because the individual has to get used to an almost entirely different way of life. The drug-using lifestyle had provided much of the meaning, structure and content of the addict's life, often for many years, then all of a sudden it is gone and something has to take its place. In short, the individual has to learn to live a new life outside the context of the drug-using environment, which had defined and structured so much of his or her existence.

Re-entering conventional life is, for most addicts, far from easy and at first they often feel strange, incompetent and lacking in important practical and social skills. This incapacity is largely a product of a cultural strangeness caused by years of detachment from mainstream culture and activities. As a result, recovering addicts often have to re-learn important aspects of conventional living. For example, for one former addict it was almost like starting life again as a baby.

> It's like you're reborn an' you've got to learn everything almost over again.
>
> *(Alison)*

The transition to a drug-free life is further complicated for some individuals by the fact that, at first, they find it difficult to function adequately without drugs. They have become so accustomed to doing almost everything while under the influence of the various drugs they have been using that, without these drugs, even the most basic of tasks can appear daunting.

As I say, I didn't know any other way o' life than drugs. When I eventually went into treatment I didn't know how to go for a pint of milk unless I had drugs in me. I wasn't able to do simple things like get up and have a bath or have a shower, brush ma teeth unless I had drugs in me. I couldn't do anythin' without drugs. So, as I said, it was all like startin' learning all over again, startin' from scratch.

(Dorothy)

The second thing that makes managing the transition out of drugs so difficult for addicts is the unrelenting nature of the task of ensuring that they remain abstinent. For recovering addicts, deciding and ceasing to take drugs is clearly not the end of the matter. A long and arduous road lies ahead strewn with pitfalls which can all too easily catch the individual out and lead to their re-addiction and re-incorporation within the drug-using world. In other words, their abstinence has to be constantly managed and sustained. However, not only is this task a constant one, it is also enduring and, while the struggle to resist the temptation of drugs tends to become less intense with the passage of time, it is something which probably never goes away completely.

The most fundamental task, which the addict has to accomplish in managing the transition from addiction to conventional life, is the establishment of a renewed identity. This, in turn, needs to be grounded in non-drug-using activities and sets of relationships. Our study suggests that two related processes are essential to the success of this enterprise: (1) addicts have to distance themselves from their former lives and, in particular, their drug-using networks, and (2) they have to develop a range of new activities and relationships both to replace those that they have given up and to reinforce and sustain their new identities. We begin by examining the ways in which the recovering addicts in our study attempted to achieve the first of these.

Avoidance of the drug-using network

There was universal agreement among our sample that, in order to give up drugs successfully, addicts had to dissociate themselves entirely from their drug-using friends and from the world of drugs. Despite having stopped, they still felt highly vulnerable and very uncertain about their ability to withstand the temptations that would be posed by exposure to the drug subculture. Accordingly, avoiding contact with drug users constituted an essential element in our recovering addicts' strategies for remaining drug-free.

> I was staying in a lot, staying away from people, keeping out of the environment because you can't stay in the environment and not take drugs. It's just not possible.
>
> *(Graham)*

> You know for me it's impossible for any individual, unless they're really, really strong, to lose a habit when they're hangin' about with . . . junkie pals, you know, people they score off. It's imposs- ible, there's too much temptation there. I knew if I was goin' to come off I knew I had to just cut out my whole circle of friends . . . I had to lose these guys.
>
> *(Frank)*

The problem was that, while the desire to overcome their addiction might be genuine and strong, the lure of the drug – and, to some extent, of the drug-using world – remained powerful. All of our recovering addicts were agreed that, once you have been addicted, the desire for drugs never went away completely, although the strength of the craving did usually abate with the passage of time.

> Some days I'll feel the urge to go an' get it, I want it. It just never leaves you really, always on your mind. We've just got to try an' work at other things, to not give up and go away and say, fuck it, I'm going to go and get a bag.
>
> *(Susie)*

> I get the same problem every morning. I'm dyin' for a hit every morning when I get up. So I give myself a slap in the face when I'm shavin' and say, 'that's the only hit you're getting'.
>
> *(Jimmy)*

It was this continuing desire for drugs that lay at the heart of the recovering addicts' sense of vulnerability. Quite simply, they had little or no confidence in their ability to resist the temptation to use again should the opportunity present itself.

Smack is a very risky thing, I don't know how I'd react if somebody gave me a half gram of smack and a set of works. I honestly don't know to this day, it's never happened to me. Five years clean or not, I honestly don't know if I would be strong enough to say 'no I can't take that' and I hope it never ever happens to me.

(Mary)

It's hard to come off and it's very, very hard to stay off because when you walk out that street and you meet somebody that's got £30 in their pocket and they're wantin' to take you for a hit, it's hard to say no . . . if somebody comes up and says, 'Look I've got a bottle of meth here', and I've been strung out for the last 10 days, I'm goin' to take that, I know I'm goin' to take it. And I don't want that.

(Tina)

The dangers of giving in to temptation were heightened by the fact that the great majority of the people we interviewed believed that, if they were to succumb, even once, it would lead inevitably to their re-addiction. As far as they were concerned, they could not use drugs intermittently, nor could they afford to dabble. It was a clear choice between abstinence or addiction.

I know if I take that one I'll not stop it, that's me I know I won't, 'cos I love drugs, I've always loved drugs, know what I mean? I was like I was mourning when I gave up drugs, it was like a loved one had died 'cos that was number one in my life. I feel as if it's not a part of my life anymore. I don't want it to be a part but I'll always think about it, just like someone dying, you always think about it.

(Judy)

Oh aye, the temptation has been there, it's been there in front of me sort of thing. It's been there in front of me and I've knocked it back. I've said 'not for me', 'cos I know if I do it once I'll be back to square one again.

(Martin)

The problem for the recovering addicts was not that their residual desire for drugs would lead them to actively go in search of them. Most of them believed that they could control these desires as long as they remained detached from the supply and use of drugs. The danger lay in situations in which drugs were readily accessible or, even worse, being used. In such situations, the addicts believed that their resolve could crumble all too easily. In the following extract, Linda describes how the smell of drugs being used came close to breaking her resolve.

Q   You say you wouldn't like to be in a context where heroin is being used?

R   Because I think it would be too tempting. It would be tempting me into sayin', 'Well just give me a wee bit, it'll not do any harm'. But I know in ma head it would. I was in that situation only, I think, about a year ago and I could smell it, I could, I knew I could smell it gettin' burnt, and I was fighting with myself not to ask for a bit, so I know that to be in a room with people doing that is really, really tempting. And that was just with the smell.

(Linda)

Indeed, so powerful is the lure of drugs that, for one former addict, even being driven through the environment in which she had fed and sustained her addiction evoked feelings of extreme vulnerability.

I go back to Glasgow to visit people with the guy I'm goin' out with now. I go back to visit his Mum and Dad, but I don't go back to Parkhead. When I do go back through Parkhead in a car I feel sick, I shake, basically I look straight ahead 'cos I don't want to see anybody at all. Parkhead is a very risky area for me. It's important to me that I don't put myself at risk where I know smack is and I know that Glasgow is a very high-risk place. What I do is we go through by car and I just go into ma boyfriend's mother's and straight back home again. I don't spend any time at all in Glasgow. Or if we stay overnight, we stay in their house in Carmyle, which is quite near Parkhead, but I don't go into Parkhead at all, I wouldn't go into Parkhead for any reason at all.

(Mary)

Clearly, from the point of view of the addict seeking to recover from addiction, their former drug-using environment contained a number of potential hazards to that recovery. The obvious solution, as far as the addicts in our study were concerned, was to endeavour to remove themselves from risk by putting as much distance as possible – socially and physically – between themselves and those who might seek to tempt or pressurise them into using again. The recovering addicts in our sample went to considerable lengths to avoid encountering their former friends. For most of them, the preferred and most common option was to move out of the area in which their drug-using career had been spent.

> It was important to get right out of the environment because the drugs were still around us and I think my weakness would have led [me] to keep usin'. So I think if I got out of the environment it was like out of sight, out of mind really, that's what I was thinkin'. 'Cos I used to say that to myself, 'I'll never get off it if I stay here'. It was all the drug people that were in my circle at the time, knocking on ma door, I couldn't sort of escape them. If I walked out on the street, they were there, if I went to cash ma giro they were there, if I went down to ma Mum's they were there, the shops, any place I went, they were there. It was always, 'are you wantin' this, are you wantin' that, so and so's got this, he's got this', know. Like I say, ma environment was a big weakness for me.
>
> *(Malky)*

Some decided to move to another town to put even more distance between themselves and their former life. The advantage of this sort of relocation was that it reduced further the chances of unwelcome encounters with drug-using acquaintances. Kate was even prepared to exchange a pleasant environment in the small town of Brechin for the 'worst area in Dundee' in order to achieve her goal.

> Q So how did you manage to come off?
>
> R I came to Dundee. I left Brechin totally, left it all behind.
>
> Q What did you leave behind?
>
> R A really nice house and the security of a nice place to live. Brechin was a nice place to live and we came into the worst area in Dundee, 'cos that was where they were willing to

give us a house. And that's the way I like it. I just changed everythin', I changed it all.

(Kate)

However, moving to another area was no guarantee that drugs could be avoided altogether. In fact, the latter are now so pervasive that it would be surprising if this were the case. For instance, Laura reported that, during a previous attempt at recovery when she had relocated to a drug-free environment, drug users had in time moved into very close proximity to her new home with the result that she eventually got involved with drugs again.

That was the first time I had ever got a house and at first the folk there were OK. Then it started getting polluted with users and I just found myself looking for it again and gettin' involved with them. I mean, there was a part of me looked for it but I tried everything in my power to avoid it. I just found it to be too inviting.

(Laura)

What moving did achieve, though, was to reduce the likelihood of encounters with people who knew the recovering addict's biography and might, for that reason, have attempted to persuade them to return to their former ways. That sort of immediate temptation was less likely in a situation in which the individual was not known as a former drug user. However, while relocation was the preferred option of most of the addicts in our study, not all of them possessed the resources, or received the necessary assistance – for example, in relation to obtaining altern-ative accommodation – to be able to move to another area or town. For the majority of our interviewees, reducing their contact with former drug-using associates and friends had to be accomplished while con-tinuing to live within the environment in which their drug-using career had evolved. For some, the solution was to venture out only at times when they knew that the chance of an unwelcome encounter with users was minimal. Others, like Graham, coped by spending as much time as possible indoors.

... keeping away from people, staying in the house, locking myself in a room I just knew that I couldn't go out, I can't go out, I have to stay in here and I have to make myself stay in here. I did it for weeks and weeks and weeks and weeks and weeks and weeks.

(Graham)

Some of these strategies might appear extreme to the outsider but they were considered by those who pursued them to be absolutely vital to their efforts to remain drug-free. They believed that they could not afford to risk the slightest contact with those who used or dealt in drugs. Although it could be very difficult, these attempts to shut addicts and dealers out of their lives did appear to work. In time, their former associates got the message, realised that their efforts to maintain or restore contact with the recovering addict were futile and gave up the attempt. It was clear from our sample's accounts of previous attempts to abstain that the price of failure to detach oneself from the drug-using environment was high. A number of our interviewees reported that remaining in, or returning to, the area in which they had pursued their habit had contributed in a major way to previous relapses.

My idea was to get away from the environment which was quite successful, I actually did quite well, but as soon as I got back to my own environment I found myself back to, 'cos I had all these friends, acquaintances I knew and I had nothin' outside that so it wasn't so much peer pressure, I'd never felt I was under peer pressure, it was more to do with my physical need for the stuff, which when you think I was off it for eight month, I could physically do without it, but as soon as you were in the environment there were triggers, you know places I seen, places I go, times I'd been in certain pubs that day, it could be anythin'.

(Roy)

Q   Why do you think you did start again?

R   I think it was a case of really, it was just what everybody else was doin', know, who you go about with. Maybe if I'd moved back to a different scheme [housing estate], but I got the exact same house back so I was with the same people an' just fell into that again.

(Paddy)

Although it can be difficult to achieve, it is possible for recovering addicts to cut themselves off from drugs entirely. Interestingly, some of our interviewees contrasted this situation with that of smoking where it is not possible to detach oneself quite so effectively. The sale and use of cigarettes is ubiquitous and very much 'in your face' and, indeed, up your nose. For that reason, some of them claimed that they had found stopping smoking harder than giving up opiates.

> I'm trying to stop smoking just now, which is harder than heroin and anything else I've tried. The problem with cigarettes is that you can't get away from the environment. You go to the pub and it's just, it's there, it's a social drug, it's becoming more anti-social right enough, but it's a social drug.
>
> *(Angus)*

> I thought I can give up, I've given up heroin, I can give up nicotine you know. Well actually no, it was easier to give up heroin because you can distance yourself from it. It's not available on every street corner, it's not socially acceptable.
>
> *(Helen)*

The interesting thing about this in the present context is the way in which the comparison provides an excellent illustration of the strength of the addicts' beliefs in the seductive power of exposure to drugs and of how important it is to avoid such exposure during attempts to recover from addiction of any sort.

Avoidance and identity reconstruction

It is important to recognise that, in attempting to distance themselves from their former life and the people who inhabited it, our recovering addicts were not simply seeking to remove themselves from temptation, although, of course, that was a vital part of what they were trying to do. Crucially, their attempt to dissociate themselves from their old friends and haunts was also about constructing new and entirely different lives for themselves. More particularly, they wanted to establish new identities. The simple fact is that they would not be able to do that successfully, if at all, if they retained the trappings of their former life and contact with it. Changing one's identity meant moving out of the drug world which had sustained that identity and which would, almost inevitably, compromise and undermine any attempt to construct a new one.

Importantly, for this process to succeed, it was vital that the recovering addict's claim to a new identity be accepted by his or her significant others (positive reinforcement), otherwise the whole enterprise could easily disintegrate. Certainly, rejection of the individual's claim to a new identity, or not being able to shed the stigma of his or her former self (negative reinforcement), could be very destructive. One way of attempting to ensure positive feedback on their new definition of self was for the addicts to move to somewhere where they were not recognised and where their past was concealed. This had the effect of removing the stigma of being known as a former addict and, thereby, assisting in the building of a new identity. For example, Steve moved to a town where he was not known for precisely that reason. He knew that the new identity that he wished to establish could be seriously threatened if his career as an addict came to be known and, accordingly, moved to a place where he would not have to live with the constant fear of having his cover blown.

Q   Why another town, what's wrong with Dundee?

R   My experience in Dundee hasn't been that nice, know what I mean, and wherever I go there's goin' to be somebody recognise me for what I was. It'll always come back to me. Can you imagine me gettin' a job, gettin' a good job and working fucking hard to get it and some donkey, some arsehole comes in and says, 'He's been takin' drugs, he's been in trouble with the police'. You know, it could fuck it up for us. It could do that to me. That's the way I look at it. A lot of jealous people about. A lot of them can't handle the fact I've stabilised maself, know what I mean?

(Steve)

For Brenda, similar considerations were at work.

Q   Why did you want to move to Edinburgh?

R   Because I wasn't going to clean up in Glasgow, I knew too many people, too many people knew me. I didn't want that and here I've not got that, 'cos they only know me as a straight person, they don't know me as a junkie. They know me as straight Brenda, they don't know me as junkie Brenda, whereas in Glasgow that's obviously what I'm

known as. They haven't got any respect for me whereas here
I get respect an' that makes me feel good about me.

(Brenda)

Difficulties associated with avoidance

Although it was a major component of our recovering addicts' strategy
to remain drug-free, detaching themselves from the drug-using subculture was not easy. Sometimes, despite the addict's best efforts, avoiding
one's drug-using friends could be difficult. Certainly, if the individual
continued to live in the area in which their habit had been pursued,
avoidance was virtually impossible since drug-using acquaintances were
likely to be all-pervasive.

Oh yea, you never really get free o' them. You meet them here,
you meet them on the street, you can't avoid them. Every time
they see you it's 'D'you want to buy temazepam, d'you want to
buy DFs?' Once you're in this drug scene it's very difficult to
break out of it . . . everywhere you go you're banging into them
you know . . . I'm meetin' them here, I'm meetin' them out on the
street, no matter where you go. It's very difficult to break out of
that circle.

(Kenny)

The fragility of the recovering addict's de-addiction is such that even
chance encounters with addict friends can be very risky.

You know you bump into somebody and that's the way it
happened. I bumped into someone and went and had a hit, and
it was just as easy as that. And it was just by chance, meetin'
somebody on the street. It was just somebody on the street who
said they had a shit-hot bit of smack and I just wanted some.

(Kate)

Being fully aware of the dangers inherent in any contact with former
friends, the recovering addict would usually endeavour to keep any such
encounters as brief as possible in an effort to preclude the emergence of
any temptation.

Aye, I had to cut myself completely off, just not see them any more. If I do see them it's just maybe hello in passing, that'll be it, 'cos I can't afford to get involved with it.

(Sharon)

I didn't go near them, just in case I did start takin' things. I'm easily influenced that way, know if they offer me things and that. So I know not to go near them. If I see them in the town now and then I'll chat to them, but that's about it. I don't want to go anywhere else with them. Keep away from anythin' like that.

(Scott)

However, the danger in encountering former acquaintances does not reside solely in the recovering addict's susceptibility to the temptations of drugs. Our interviewees were also very much aware that some of their addict 'friends' would seek deliberately to undermine their efforts to abstain partly, perhaps, out of a genuine desire to regain their companionship but more likely out of envy for their achievement in giving up. Linda described the desire of addicts to bring the former user down in the following way.

And then a lot o' folk as well don't like to see you comin' off drugs 'cos that's the way drugs make your mind work. You don't want to see anybody off drugs, you want everybody down with you.

(Linda)

Some of our interviewees clearly felt more resilient and did not experience the same need to avoid the company of their former friends. For them, the crucial thing was to stay away from situations in which drugs were actually being used.

Q   So did you make a conscious decision to stay away from people that were using heavy drugs?

R   Well I made a decision to stay away from them while they were usin', I didn't mind going about with them in town or that but I made a decision to stay away from the houses that were involved.

(Dennis)

A few reported being able to keep the company of users as long as they remained disciplined and exited when drugs were about to be used.

> I find I've always gone back to the same friends again after four or five years when I'm better. But sitting watching them take out drugs and various other things and watching them taking has the same effect on me as the sea does on the shore. It just wears you away and wears you away until eventually you just collapse and subside. The best method of prevention for me is to remember if I'm sitting in the company and somebody says 'I'm goin' to be takin'. . . heroin . . .' is to say, 'well hold on', and I just go away and leave them to it.
>
> *(Jimmy)*

We should emphasise, however, that those who believed they could maintain contact with drug-using acquaintances and remain drug-free were very much in the minority. Most of our sample subscribed to the view that the only way to be sure of not succumbing to temptation was to detach yourself completely from drugs and their use.

Although current users were clearly best avoided by those seeking to recover from addiction, this did not mean that contact with them was always negative in its effect. According to some of our sample, seeing people under the influence of drugs, and being reminded of the squalor and degradation associated with the lifestyle, could actually serve to strengthen their resolve to sustain their recovery.

> The more I see somebody stoned, the more I don't want it, the more I go, 'God I was like that'. I get embarrassed not for them but for me 'cos I was like that at one time.
>
> *(Paula)*

However, former friends were not the only source of exposure to illegal drugs in our interviewees' social circles. It was also quite common for relatives, including members of their own immediate families, to be involved in drug-taking as well. When this happened, it was even more problematic for the recovering addicts than the threat posed by their former drug-using networks. The recovering addicts could disengage from friends much more readily than they could dissociate themselves from family members: firstly, the social ties are stronger with the latter and, secondly, there is often a problem of physical proximity when an individual actually lives with members of his or her own family. Nevertheless, insofar as they could, the recovering addicts in our study sought to avoid the company of family members – usually brothers, sisters or cousins – who were users.

> I don't visit ma family. I don't go to ma brother's for the reason he's using, 'cos we were partners for using . . . he's lived with me all his life, used with me, d'you know what I mean?
>
> *(Nancy)*

> Ma whole family just about are on drugs. But I don't have an awful lot to do with them. I mean I still care about ma family but I just tend not to go near them.
>
> *(Linda)*

What was much more difficult for the individual seeking to come off drugs was if their partner was also a user. This, in fact, was quite common since the socially constraining nature of the drug-using lifestyle severely restricted opportunities to develop relationships with non-users, thereby increasing the likelihood that the partners of addicts would also be using drugs. The problem, of course, with trying to quit when their partners were using was that there was no escape from drugs and the temptation to use; the recovering addicts were continually exposed to it in the context of their own homes.

> At times it was difficult 'cos sometimes he would bring people in and take hits in the house and sometimes he'd put it right in front of ma nose. He'd bring people in to cut kit and put it in bags . . . it was difficult.
>
> *(Rhona)*

In addition to exposing them to temptation, partners who continued to use drugs would also sometimes apply pressure on the recovering addict to take up the habit again. For instance, Amanda had to pretend that she was still using in order to avoid her boyfriend's wrath.

> I had to pretend I was takin' drugs so that he'd be OK, because he was gettin' really mad when he realised that I wasn't takin' drugs, he was gettin' mad that I was coming off and he never had whatever it was to do it.
>
> *(Amanda)*

On the other hand, a drug-using partner could sometimes facilitate and strengthen an addict's attempt to recover from addiction where a couple agreed to try to give up drugs at the same time. Such 'abstinence pacts' were not uncommon and could assist the effort to quit quite considerably through mutual support and reinforcement. In addition, of course, as Jane explained, it also meant that a major source of temptation was removed.

> This is the first time that the two of us have ever gone together at the same time for help. So now neither of us has got smack about us so I'm findin' it a wee bit easier. Whereas, if he hadn't gone for help, he'd still have been takin' it so I would have been coming back home and it would be in the house.
>
> *(Jane)*

It was, however, not always possible for the addicts who sought to recover to get the support and compliance of their partners and sometimes decisive action had to be taken if the latter were not to destroy their efforts to abstain. For example, Barbara concluded that she had no alternative but to evict her drug-using partner in order to protect herself and give her attempt to come off drugs a realistic chance of success.

> My man he was still using an' I ended up kicking him out because of it 'cos I didn't want to end up getting full of it. Yea, that's what I did, kicked him out so I did. 'Cos I'm not having that around me or the bairn.
>
> *(Barbara)*

Disengaging from one's partner was far from easy and, more commonly, the addict attempting to exit drug misuse found it difficult, or even impossible, to achieve. A frequent outcome of such failure was re-addiction.

Drug users of one sort or another are not the only problem as far as putting temptation in the recovering addict's way is concerned. A bigger problem for a considerable number of our interviewees was the efforts which dealers would make to try to persuade them to continue their habit. Drug dealers clearly have a strong vested interest in preventing successful recovery since addicts constitute their livelihood. Accordingly, they would often go to considerable lengths to achieve their ends. This included offering the recovering addicts free drugs and even turning up on their doorsteps to proffer their wares.

The biggest problem is you're giving somebody money all the time and when you stop takin' it they don't like not gettin' that money. So they're like, 'How's it going, there's a gram for nothing.' A guy turned up at my door once and he was like 'We got a new K of speed in, a new guy making and that, d'you want to try it out for us?' Know what I mean 'cos I was experienced in takin' speed and they knew if I took a gram of it and I was speedin' out of ma head with it, it was good sulph, know what I mean? So we'll call him Ramsay. So he's like that, 'There's a quarter bag for nothing', you know. So I ended up gettin' back into it again after packing it in over a period of three weeks.

(Peter)

Since I've stopped, the amount of drugs I've been offered for nothin' are phenomenal. I mean I've never been offered drugs for nothin' and now I'm not takin' them they're giving me them. And I've spent say six months saying what the hell do they all want to offer me drugs for and I know there's only one solution. They want my money, they want me to go back the same way that I was. They were as addicted to my £120 a day as I was to their £120 worth of heroin a day.

(Jimmy)

In their highly vulnerable state, having drugs thrust at them was the last thing that the recovering addicts needed and the sort of pressure we have described could make someone struggling to overcome their addiction feel very threatened and sometimes, as in Colin's case, very angry.

Well, like dealers and I mean the phone calls or people at your door, I'm still getting it now, two years after. I had a guy at half-past-nine at the door. By half-past-nine at night, he'd obviously overspent his money and he'd come to try his luck. This used to happen often, it only happens once in a blue moon now. But he came to the door and he's asking 'd'you want this, d'you want that'. I was like if he'd been a bit straighter or had more sense I would've hooked him . . . He's twenty-five, he's only young, but he's a real arsehole. He's the type of guy that really deserves the chop because he pushes it on people, you know he's already been in jail for sellin' an' dealin' to young people. And I can't stand it, you know, because they know the vulnerability. And I said, 'Look you really shouldn't, I mean I know where you are and if I need it, I'll come to you. You start comin' to my door you're really pushing it, you're not a dealer you're a pusher.' It's just, it was good, I was happy that I was able to act in that way because I had the money, I could have had it if I wanted.

(Colin)

Not surprisingly, dealers were at the top of each recovering addict's list of people to be avoided. Unfortunately, this was not always easy in an area replete with illegal drugs and those trading in them.

Stay away from the dealers, not easy round here . . . We have one staying next door, one stays in the next block, there's one stays across there and another across the road from him so within about twenty yards there's four or five dealers.

(Gordon)

In addition to the difficulties involved in avoiding drug-using friends and relatives, success in achieving this could in itself give rise to problems. In particular, it could lead to social isolation because, until an alternative network of non-users was established, the recovering addict could find him or herself devoid of friends and social contact. Frequently, as in Michael's case, the only people the recovering addicts knew were users and the only venues they were familiar with were places where addicts congregated.

But in avoiding them what happens is because that was my whole lifestyle I find myself not going anywhere, not doing anything . . . the only places I know are for users.

(Michael)

This situation was frequently compounded by the fact that the addicts would often have become detached from their own families as a consequence of their addiction. Sometimes they would simply have drifted away from them but, in other instances, their family might have 'disowned' them. In either case, it usually took time for meaningful contact to be re-established. All of this could create a social void in the addict's life and the loneliness and lack of support that resulted could make the individual's efforts to quit that much more difficult and could, at worst, contribute to the recovering addict deciding to start taking drugs again.

For example, Douglas lost his girlfriend who had constituted his only contact with the straight world and, as a result, returned to the company of users and to drugs.

> Well I was still in the same place, the same environment if you like and although I was seein' a girl I fell out with her, so I had nothin' to do and all my friends were all drug addicts so I had no friends, no girlfriend. I ended up goin' to see one of ma old friends for something to do and ended up taking it once. Then, 'Oh I'll take it again 'cos I can get away with it 'cos I'm not addicted to it.' And before you know it you've got a habit.
>
> *(Douglas)*

Social isolation can be a particular problem when addicts decide to move town in an attempt to assist their recovery. If addicts have few, or no, contacts in another town, the loneliness and isolation of being on their own in a strange city can result in their seeking company and comfort where they know they will gain ready acceptance – that is, in the drug-using world. Three of our sample gave this as the main reason for previous relapses.

> I don't know why I started usin' but it was a strange city for me and I didn't know anybody and it's hard to meet people that are straight in a place like this. It was the loneliness. Eventually I went back to the drugs and drink.
>
> *(Catriona)*

The fact that social isolation can contribute to relapse demonstrates the importance of the recovering addict establishing an alternative set of social relationships as quickly as possible. This is a theme to which we return later in the chapter.

Developing new activities and relationships

While dissociating oneself from one's former friends and drug-using lifestyle is a vital ingredient of any addict's attempt to come off drugs, this is not in itself sufficient to ensure that the individual will remain abstinent and not relapse. It is also essential that the recovering addict replace his or her former life with a new set of non-drug-related activities and relationships. There are two reasons why this is important. Firstly, the great majority of former addicts need to fill the void in their lives that giving up drugs creates. Secondly, these new activities and relationships provide the basis upon which a new identity can be fashioned and preserved. We begin by considering the filling of the void.

Filling the void: occupying one's time

One of the main problems which addicts face when they give up drugs is that of how to occupy their time. The drug-using routine – getting the money, acquiring the drug and taking the drug – had previously absorbed a major part of their day. Then, all of a sudden, they find that these activities have gone and that they have a lot of time on their hands. The danger with this is that idleness and boredom might expose them to the temptation of taking drugs again.

> But you get dead bored with it. And you're that used to for years running about and scoring and that, that's been your life, then all of a sudden there's nothin' to do anymore. I think that's how a lot of them start using again, pure boredom.
>
> (Barbara)

The recovering addicts we interviewed were well aware of the importance of filling this gap in their lives and were clear that one of the best antidotes to the temptation to return to drugs was to keep themselves as fully occupied as possible, both mentally and physically.

> If you've got somethin' to do, that's a good substitute to help you come off drugs. You can't just come off drugs and sit and do nothin'. If you've got somethin' constructive to do, hobbies or somethin', that gives you somethin' to concentrate on, to blank out the drugs.
>
> (Marion)

Taking away the drugs you have to fill the gaps and it's a huge gap because if you're not out stealing you're away scoring and away hitting up. If you take that away from a drug-user's life, you're leavin' them with nothin'. Absolutely nothin'. So you have to fill these gaps so they feel good, so they don't have to say, 'Right I want to feel good, I know what makes me feel good, a hit'. And that's what you have to do, you have to fill the gaps.

(Mary)

So, how did the recovering addicts seek to occupy their time? Well, at the most basic level, it was simply a matter of finding things to do that were unrelated to drugs and which filled their days. Almost anything would suffice as long as it provided the necessary distraction. For example, Sharon filled her days with domestic chores.

Initially I was in the house all the time. Sitting watching the TV or whatever or sitting listening to [music]. But I've started taking on a lot of responsibility for just basically lookin' after the house. I take everything to do with this house, know what I mean? My Mam's gettin' old, she's looked after me all ma life and what I basically did to fill in ma days would be get up in the morning and do the chores that needed done in ma house. Maybe going out and getting in what's needed for that day, walkin' the dog and basically your day can get filled doing these sort of things.

(Sharon)

However, for most of the individuals in our study, simply occupying their time was not enough, important though that was. Many of them expressed the view that having something to do was also an important way of infusing their life with a sense of purpose – in other words, of giving it meaning. In short, it was not enough to simply be occupied; the activities in which one engaged had, ideally, to be purposive and rewarding. For four of our sample going to college provided the solution to finding a way of occupying their time that was also fulfilling. A larger number turned to voluntary work. Frequently this involved helping other drug addicts since this was an area in which they felt particularly well qualified to make a contribution.

The ideal solution for our sample of recovering addicts was paid employment. Not only did this impose very full demands and a strict discipline on the individual – and thereby help to keep them out of mischief – it was also particularly effective in imparting meaning to their lives and securing for them a stake in the future. According to Bernadette it was essential to her recovery.

I still kept my same job. I think if I hadn't been workin' I think I would have probably stuck it two days . . . I wasn't thinking, 'Oh how am I going to get to sleep the night', I was thinking, 'I hope I get a couple of hours sleep so I can get up for work'. So I had something to focus on. If I wasn't working, I don't think I'd have lasted two days, I think I'd have been away chasin' drugs again.

(Bernadette)

For the majority of our interviewees, securing paid employment was far from easy. In addition to any concerns which a prospective employer might have as to whether the individual really had overcome their drug use, there was also the problem that the recovering addict was likely to have been out of the job market for a lengthy period.

If you've had long-term drug addiction behind you, you're out of the work place. I mean you're out of it for a decade. You try gettin' back in again. That's another reason why people find the last lap the hardest of all.

(Fiona)

Filling the void: replacing social relationships

Another sense in which there is a void to be filled is that the former addict needs to replace the social relationships which their drug-using lifestyle had previously supplied and which they have now abandoned. Our interviewees were well aware of the disingenuousness and fickleness of the majority of these relationships and, indeed, many remarked on how a fellow addict could never be a true friend because of the extreme self-centredness and dishonesty that pervades the drug subculture. Nevertheless those individuals did provide them with companionship, a sense of belonging and support of a kind and these were things that members of our sample sometimes missed when they severed their connections with the group. They would describe feeling lonely and isolated when parted from their former friends and of missing the sense of comfort and acceptance that went with membership of the group. Some even went so far as to describe their addict friends as being like a 'family' to them. For Nancy the comfort and security of the group were such that she even wondered if losing her friends was a price worth paying for coming off drugs.

Well all ma pals still used. So as much as I was trying to stay away from them I still needed the contact, it was like a safety thing for me. Although they were all using and I wasn't I felt safe within that group. I knew I could talk ma mind within that group and nobody would laugh. Everybody was sort of, 'we know what you're talking about', d'you know what I mean? That was like a family for me, all the users were like ma family, that's how I saw it. I was so comfortable within ma own wee group. I don't have any friends now since coming off drugs. Sometimes that crosses ma mind, is it worth it? Being straight but not having any pals. I've got myself and I've got the guy I live with and ma kids, you know what I mean? Sometimes I ask myself, 'Is it enough, am I looking for more than that?'

(Nancy)

The feeling of comfort which many of our interviewees felt within the context of their relationships with other drug users was often contrasted with the sense of strangeness and distance which they experienced within the context of their evolving relationships with non-drug users.

If you're in a crowd that all smoke cannabis or take heroin or drink heavy or take Valium you feel normal. If you move out o' that environment, then you feel odd, you feel strange . . . you're not comfortable, so you want to be in that comfortable situation.

(Robin)

Given what we have just described, there was always a danger that a desire for positive social contact could, if not satisfied elsewhere, entice the addict to return to the bosom of their former friends and, eventually, to their drug-using lifestyle.

The role of activities and relationships in identity renewal

So, filling the social and occupational vacuum created by giving up drugs is one reason why it is important for the recovering addict to develop a new set of activities and relationships. The second reason is that this is an essential component of any attempt to build and sustain a new identity. The latter has to be grounded in activities and relationships which reinforce it by providing an alternative lifestyle, a sense of purpose and a stake in the future. Very importantly, these new practices and arrangements also have to provide positive reinforcement for the recovering addict's attempt to develop a more positive sense of self. Without the sustaining influence of a range of drug-free activities and relationships, the addiction will simply be replaced by a void; it might be a drug-free void but, since it does not reinforce and sustain a new identity, it is essentially unstable and is therefore destined to fail. The recovering addict's attempt to build a different future and sense of self has to be sustained by something more than simply coming off drugs. This requirement was well recognised by the addicts themselves. For example, one of our respondents described feeling like an 'empty shell' when he stopped using drugs.

> I couldn't get rid o' this empty feeling when I came off the drugs, know a total empty shell, just nothin'.
>
> *(Stewart)*

The recovering addicts we interviewed were well aware of the role which being occupied in a meaningful way played in establishing a new life and positive sense of self. For Catriona and Ed their hope for the future lay in further education.

> You need somethin' to keep you going, somethin' that you're determined to finish and see through ... and I'm hoping that college will do that for me, 'cos I know if I start using, college will fall apart.
>
> *(Catriona)*

> You've got to really want to get off the stuff but in order to do that you've got to have some other purpose in your life whether that be college or a job you enjoy or a girlfriend or something like that. You've got to have something to replace the drug and something quite dramatic as well . . . as I said, something that will fill up your time, something like college, plenty of homework and studying and things. Something that will actually replace that. You've got to have some sort of substance in your life I think.
>
> *(Ed)*

While engagement in non-drug-related activities was extremely important in the development of the recovering addict's new identity, his or her relationship with non-drug users was of at least equal significance in this process. Since an individual's identity is formed and maintained in interaction with significant others, positive reinforcement from other people is central to building and sustaining a new sense of self. Accordingly, the acceptance by non-addicts of the recovering addict's new identity was especially important in sustaining its development and, thereby, in maintaining the individual's abstinence from drugs. Where such acceptance was not forthcoming, or where the recovering addict's claim to a new identity was denied or disputed, the potential for relapse was considerably enhanced. Sometimes the individual's relationships with non-addicts were pre-existing – for example, with relatives and former friends – and simply had to be reactivated. However, they also frequently developed out of the recovering addict's new activities. What all this means is that finding meaningful ways of deploying their time was functional to the recovering addicts in several ways: (1) it helped them to occupy themselves and thereby provided a distraction from drugs; (2) it helped to establish a new and more positive sense of self; and (3) it often provided a new set of relationships with the potential to reinforce their new identity.

The continuing appeal of the addict lifestyle

The need for the recovering addict to find alternative activities and relationships was accentuated by the fact that their drug-using lifestyle frequently retained a considerable appeal for some of them. Inherent within this was the potential to draw them back into drug misuse if their drug-related lifestyle was not adequately replaced. We have already described how the companionship of former friends and acquaintances could be missed and the pull which this could exert on those who felt lonely, isolated or rejected within their new, drug-free world. However, the appeal of the drug-taking lifestyle was not confined to the company and sense of belonging, which addict friends provided. There were other aspects of the lifestyle, which our sample had clearly found to be enjoyable and even rewarding. For example, several of our sample volunteered that they had derived a great deal of pleasure from drugs and from the sensations which they conferred.

> I quite enjoyed it. It was really like having a lovely affair that had to end, that got too much, there was somethin' quite comforting about it.
>
> *(Helen)*

> Up until I was 21 if I had the chance to change ma life I don't think I would come off drugs because I was havin' too much of a good time really. A hell of a great time. It was brilliant.
>
> *(Douglas)*

In addition to the pleasurable effects of the drug itself, the associated lifestyle could also provide excitement and a sense of achievement. Some addicts clearly found this highly stimulating.

> But there's a bit of me that thrives on the lifestyle, the junkie bit of me . . . Actually going and getting somethin', going and getting say a bit of smack and havin' that in your hand. It's like, 'Yes, I've done it'. It's like you've achieved somethin'.
>
> *(Angela)*

> At the time all you could see in front of you was that hit. You would do anythin' at all to get it, you know what I mean? I just find it exciting . . . running about for it, the chase for it, ducking an' diving, exciting you know what I mean? It just seemed like you didn't have enough time on your hands like to go out and score. The fact of going out and chasin' an' gettin' that reward at the end of it. Just feels tremendous like.
>
> *(Dennis)*

In comparison, recovering addicts often found life without drugs to be 'boring' and 'empty' and, for that reason, difficult to adjust to.

> Because it is exciting taking drugs, you find that the normal day-to-day living is quite mundane . . . no big excitement running about here, running about there. That's a hard bit to get used to, sometimes it's like a bit boring, you know what I mean? Compared to the way you were takin' drugs.
>
> *(Bernadette)*

> See when you're not takin' anythin' your life's dead boring 'cos you're not running out scoring, takin' drugs, lookin' for drugs and that. You've got to come to terms with that as well . . . your life's pure boring, it is.
>
> *(Barbara)*

As a result, a number of our interviewees described a need to find a 'high' in other areas of life to compensate. One recovering addict referred to this as 'glamorising serenity'.

> You've got to glamorise serenity then haven't you, d'you know what I mean? To go into serenity, you've got to glamorise it haven't you . . . See when I do the aerobics it's like an hour's rave to me, know what I mean? Up there bouncing about and shouting and all the rest of it and that's glamorising it for me.
>
> *(Tracy)*

In addition to experiencing a certain sense of loss on coming off drugs – at least initially – some addicts also found that they were worse off financially as well. The activities in which they had engaged in order to support their habit had frequently produced a surplus of cash over and above what they required for drugs. In consequence, when using, the addict could sometimes feel quite well off. On the other hand, on giving up drugs their involvement in crime and prostitution also tended to cease and their financial situation suffered accordingly.

> Money is really a big problem, because with the drugs, you were takin' your whack [cut] of selling the smack, you were takin' your whack off of selling the hash, you had plenty o' money. And he [partner] was stealing as well. You had plenty o' money, you were used to havin' money and then you're back to scabby Monday book [Social Security benefits]. How am I going to live off of this? How can I buy messages [provisions] with this?
>
> *(Linda)*

By reminding us of the seductive appeal of certain aspects of a life on drugs, these accounts provide a ringing endorsement of the importance of replacing the addict's former lifestyle with activities and relationships that are both satisfying and rewarding. It is clear from our recovering addicts' accounts of unsuccessful attempts to come off drugs that failure to replace the drug-using lifestyle, or to counteract its appeal, was a major factor in their relapse.

> I've tried it a few times, but it's just boredom, there's nothin' to do. I wanted somethin' to do. I wanted to be either out working

or doing somethin' different, but there was nothin' to do, so it was just back to the drugs.

(Kevin)

I probably had about two or three feeble attempts at stopping . . . Basically when I did stop I never had any direction and boredom took me back.

(Joe)

The role of employment

Of particular importance in the process of building a drug-free life was the role played by formal employment. In addition to its part in keeping the recovering addict occupied and out of the way of temptation, it performed three other very important functions. First, it provided an escape from the world of drugs together with an alternative network of non-users to whom the recovering addict could relate and who could provide reinforcement for his or her claims to a new identity. Second, it strengthened ties to conventional society by providing the addict with a stake in the future together with the means by which he or she could sustain a drug-free lifestyle. Third, it encouraged the former addict in a positive sense of self, based on the satisfaction which he or she derived from holding down a regular job. Being able to achieve this core status was an important symbol to the individual of their ability to return successfully to a conventional life. Given what we have just described, it is not surprising that a recovering addict's inability to obtain a job could play a significant part in relapse.

I was tryin' to get a job but every time I went for an interview it was, 'No, we don't want you'. So we [interviewee and partner] started havin' petty arguments . . . 'cos I had no money, no job. So one time we had a massive argument, she's throwing things at me so I walked out of the house and I went back and had a hit.

(Brian)

The loss of employment subsequent to coming off drugs could have a similar effect.

> So I was off drugs and I had ma job and everything but when ma job packed up, I didn't realise the work must have been helping me 'cos I sank into deep depression and I just started taking whatever.
>
> *(Amanda)*

Although gaining employment following addiction was difficult, a small proportion of our sample had been able to retain jobs while they were using drugs and to hold on to them subsequently. Sometimes holding on to a job while using was difficult. However, for those who were able to achieve it, it had the advantage of keeping them out of the drug subculture and of ensuring that they retained their participation in conventional networks. This, in turn, made the transition to a drug-free life that much easier.

Too much to lose

Once they began to develop, the individuals' new lives – with their new activities, relationships and commitments – created a powerful barrier against the temptation to revert to past drug-using behaviours. There were three related aspects to this. First of all, their new lives gave them a stake in the present and an incentive to maintain it. For the recovering addicts, a stake in the present – whether it was through a job, a partner or children – and the sense of normality, well-being and positive reinforcement that this provided, was absolutely central to their ability to remain abstinent and to sustain a drug-free lifestyle. Linda expressed this in the following way.

> I'm lucky to have my husband and my kids but there's a lot of folk that don't have things like that and there's nothin' out here for them. I believe if it wasn't [for] them I'd probably be back on drugs because I know nothin' else.
>
> *(Linda)*

However, not only did these commitments help to bind the individual to the norms and dictates of conventional society, our respondents also found achievements such as holding down a job, maintaining a steady relationship, taking part in voluntary activity, having non-using friends or simply doing normal drug-free things like decorating their home tremendously rewarding. All of these activities imparted a sense of normality and progress to the individual and helped to reinforce his or her faith both in the desirability and in the probable success of their rehabilitation. Sometimes what might appear to be quite small achievements could contribute significantly to this sense of satisfaction and progress.

> Well I'm decorating ma hall now. Ma house was a mess, a complete tip. Everythin' was lying about, but it's spotless now. It's like a boost 'cos I can feel myself lifting myself back up off the ground, know what I mean?
>
> (Tina)

In turn, the rewards which they derived from their new lives gradually stiffened the recovering addicts' resolve to remain abstinent and hardened their resistance to drugs.

> You start havin' money and that, you can go back out and start buying clothes again. It feels better. Once you feel the benefits of it, it feels a lot better than when you were pure mad with it . . . I prefer this life to the one I had. I wouldn't mess it up.
>
> (Barbara)

> Starting work, getting a bit o' pay, I went to Jamaica on ma honeymoon. All these different things picked me up and kept me up, know, as far as drugs.
>
> (Alastair)

> Oh it was great, great to feel dead fit, able to do a lot more things. I thought I'd just be lazy all the time, but I wasn't, know, I was out and about. I'm proud of myself doin' what I've done. It was a big achievement for me, I do feel proud comin' off them 'cos I didn't ever think I'd do it, honestly never. I was dead chuffed with myself, it gave me a great feelin' inside.
>
> (Scott)

Sometimes our interviewees would consciously remind themselves of what taking up drugs again would mean for them and how much they stood to lose by doing so. For Jane it meant thinking about what her recidivism would mean for her children.

> The other night I was tempted. A lassie I know was goin' to get a bit. And when she said it I knew I could have went with her and took that wee bit. If I hadn't had ma wee lassie with me, I think I might have. But I just kept lookin' at ma wee lassie and said 'No, I need to go', and I walked away from her.
>
> *(Jane)*

The second thing that their new lives provided for the recovering addicts was a stake in the future. One of the things that their drug-using lifestyle had done was to foreclose on their future by limiting their horizon to their next hit and preventing them from seeing a life beyond drugs. Once they came off drugs, however, a new life became possible and individuals could, once again, begin to envisage a future for themselves and to plan for it. Our sample were all agreed that a belief in a positive and sustainable future was of great importance for their continued recovery.

> I'll maybe have a job. I'll be able to do more things wi' ma lass an' ma bairn. Be able to go places, go on holiday an' that, something that I've never been able to do because all ma money's gone in ma arm. Be able to buy things. I've passed ma test [driving] now, I could think about gettin' a car, maybe get married, I'll just see what happens.
>
> *(Kevin)*

It was largely the prospect of being able to maintain and develop a worthwhile life without drugs that made abstinence worthwhile. Without that there would have been much less incentive for the recovering addicts to remain drug-free. For some, even, a bleak future without drugs might have been perceived as being little better, or perhaps even worse, than a life of addiction. The importance of the activities and relationships that constituted the recovering addicts' restored lives was that these provided them with the means by which they could maintain their belief in a positive and, importantly, an enduring future. They could now see the prospect of a satisfying and rewarding future where previously there had been none.

The third function that the recovering addicts' new lives performed was to confirm and reinforce their new identities as non-addicts and as useful members of society. The various components of their reconstructed lives promoted in the individuals a positive sense of themselves as people who could make a valuable contribution to society and who could build and maintain effective relationships with others. In short, they helped the recovering individuals to regain their self-respect and sense of worth. As we have argued, this process of restoring a spoiled identity would appear to be crucial to successful recovery from addiction. For this reason, their renewed identities were highly prized by the members of our sample and considered much too precious to lose.

> All your motivation, self-respect, self-confidence, self-esteem are non-existent when you've got a habit and it's very, very hard to get that back. When it does come back you feel good, and you don't want to lose it.
>
> *(Tom)*

> I have gained a lot o' self-respect for myself as a straight person and a lot o' confidence for myself. And all the self-respect and confidence I had as a user was just all false, it wasn't real. I like myself as a straight person better than I did when I was a user . . . I find myself it's important to be clean to achieve the things that I want to achieve and not to be a victim anymore.
>
> *(Maria)*

In the context of their new identity, our recovering addicts frequently expressed revulsion at their former drug-using lifestyle. According to them, this perception helped to strengthen their resolve never to use drugs again.

> I don't want the hassle an' the lifestyle an' the muck that goes along with it. I couldn't go back to all that, in an' out of jail. It's just not a life. It's just an existence among other drug addicts, that's all.
>
> *(Lorna)*

In retrospect, Sally was 'sickened' at the thought of her former identity and lifestyle.

 Q   What sort of environment are you trying to avoid?

R   Just the drug scene really. And I just don't want to be like that anymore, 'cos when I see them [addicts] and I see them actually falling about really stoned out their head, that really sickens me. And it sickens me to think I was like that at one time, when I was on heroin I was like that and it sickens me to think I was actually like that.

(Sally)

In time, the drug scene could come to be seen by former addicts as being foreign to them; to be part of another, and increasingly distant, existence and one to which they had no desire to return. For Judy, who had been addicted to heroin for ten years, the drug life eventually became a 'different world'.

I feel as if I don't communicate with them anymore, they're in a different world from me so I would feel awkward. Not scared that I would use, because I wouldn't use but I just feel as if they're on a different wavelength from me now and I see people stoned on buses and I go, 'I used to be like that'.

(Judy)

What all of this amounts to is that one of the most significant factors in the process of recovery from addiction would appear to be the fact that recovering addicts frequently reach a stage at which they perceive themselves as having too much to lose by returning to drugs. They have developed significant stakes in the non-using world which they are simply not prepared to jeopardise. These 'stakes' can comprise a job or other rewarding activities; important relationships with others; their improved material well-being; or, importantly, their new identity. In short, their new life and their renewed sense of self come to have a stronger appeal than the drug. Mary sums this up very well in the following extract.

There are days when I still want to get stoned. Like an hour ago I thought, 'Yea I could be doin' with getting stoned' . . . but then you know it's like I've got a tape in ma head I can play and say, 'Mary if you get stoned what are you going to lose?' and that's it. But back then I didn't . . . But I think when you're further down the line you do start thinking about all the other stuff, no I didn't want to lose ma job, no I didn't want to lose ma kids, I didn't want to lose myself. But if I go away and get a hit that would make me feel shit about myself and even being clean nearly five years it still puts me back to square one for taking that hit. I've got this job where people do look to me, I do get respect, I know with having this job what I could lose if I muck up again. So the balance I've got is like that there's so many things I could lose. Basically the main thing is losin' my self-respect, losin' my own identity and I don't want to lose that.

(Mary)

In summary, then, the more their lives and identities are restored, the more commitments they assume and the more positive their experiences of a drug-free life become, the greater is the recovering addicts' resistance to returning to drugs. As we have seen, central to this process is the individual's ability to develop a range of drug-free activities and relationships which support the construction of an alternative lifestyle and future and which help to sustain a renewed sense of self. Above all, it is being able to feel positive about oneself and one's identity and being able to see a viable and satisfying future that most sustains recovery from addiction.

Managing the desire for drugs

As we indicated earlier, a fundamental problem that has to be managed by all recovering addicts is the fact that their desire for the drug, or drugs, to which they have become addicted is never eradicated completely. However strong an addict's desire to quit, a residual longing, together with occasional cravings, remains a constant threat to their efforts to remain drug-free. This has to be dealt with if the individual is to stand any chance of succeeding in their attempt to conquer their addiction. We have already seen how nearly all of the recovering addicts in our sample attempted to manage this source of vulnerability by distancing themselves from people and places that might expose them to illegal drugs or to the practice and ritual of drug-taking. However, this was not the only method they employed in order to avoid or resist temptation. A number of other strategies were deployed and, according to our interviewees, to good effect.

One of the most common devices was the substitution of the drug to which they had been addicted by some other drug or substance. The recovering addicts frequently felt the need to fill the gap left by their former drug use, especially in the early stages of de-addiction. Substitution usually took the form of using alcohol or cannabis as a way of achieving an alternative 'high', although other drugs, such as temazepam, were sometimes used for this purpose as well. The literature on de-addiction suggests that this device is widely employed by recovering addicts with alcohol and cannabis being the most commonly employed substitutes (Waldorf 1983, Biernacki 1986, Christo 1998). However, this strategy is not without its dangers and four of our sample reported replacing their drug habit with a pattern of excessive drinking. Frykholm's work suggests that the abuse of substitute drugs might constitute a considerable problem as far as recovering addicts are concerned and reports that 'numerous studies estimate that at least 20 per cent of former addicts . . . go into heavy drinking and subsequent alcoholism or end up in a sad state of mixed abuse of alcohol, sedatives and hypnotics' (Frykholm 1985, p. 345). However, for most of our sample who used this method, it appeared that the substitute was either used only as a short-term measure to help them to get over the initial period following withdrawal or it was employed in moderation.

The other main strategy that our sample used to overcome their desire for drugs was 'distraction'. Basically, this consisted of trying to concentrate one's mind and activities on matters that were unrelated to drugs and, in this way, to attempt to squeeze all thoughts of drugs out of their consciousness. This would appear to be the most common method for dealing with unwelcome desires for a range of addictions (Stall and Biernacki 1986). Another strategy employed by members of our sample was to remind themselves of the negative side of using drugs, what Biernacki (1986) refers to as 'negative contexting'. This consisted of the former addicts reminding themselves of how awful life on drugs had been and of what they now had to lose by succumbing to temptation.

> One thing that I do keep on board is I don't forget where I came from 'cos I could quite easily end up back there in next to no time. I don't forget the way I was when I was out there using 'cos the worst day I get in recovery can be nowhere near as bad as when I was using. It's as plain and simple as that.
>
> *(Joe)*

As other researchers have observed, it is the new life that the recovering addict has built, with its new activities, commitments and relationships, that provides the raw materials for dealing with unwelcome thoughts by means of distraction or negative contexting (Stall and Biernacki 1986, Biernacki 1986). In other words, the recovering addicts manage their desire for drugs by thinking about and doing things that are related to their new identities. It is the presence of non-drug-related activities in their lives and the value which they attach to their new lifestyle and sense of self that makes these strategies so effective.

Testing one's resolve

Despite our sample's general acknowledgement of the importance of avoiding drug users and drug-using environments, paradoxically a small number of them quite deliberately exposed themselves to precisely that sort of temptation. Two of our interviewees reported that they had deliberately set out to test their resistance and resolve by placing themselves in the company of addicts. Three went further and claimed that they had actually used the drugs on which they had been dependent during their current period of abstinence, ostensibly in order to prove to themselves that they were no longer addicted. It is, of course, difficult to assess the status of such claims and the authenticity of what such action was intended to achieve. However, on the basis of these three respondents' accounts, it appeared that it was possible to take a single 'hit' without relapsing.

It would seem that such experimentation is not uncommon among recovering addicts. For example, Waldorf (1983) found that 26 per cent of his sample of former heroin addicts had 'tested' themselves in this way. Perhaps some addicts need to be reassured that they can no longer be drawn back into drugs – that they have truly broken their addiction – in order to be able to lay their addict identity to rest and move on to a new phase in their lives. It is conceivable that, in demonstrating to themselves that they can sample drugs again without becoming addicted, some addicts may acquire a sense of security which enables them to establish new lives without constantly looking over their shoulders and wondering if and when they might succumb to temptation and become re-addicted. If they can try the drug once and still remain abstinent, they may feel that they have broken its hold over them.

A more sceptical interpretation of the actions described above would be that the individuals involved were simply hoping that they could continue to use drugs on an occasional basis. If this were the case, certainly none of them was admitting to it. However, some members of our sample did confess that, during previous attempts at recovery, they had used the device of 'testing one's resistance' as a pretext for getting back into drugs full-time.

> I ended up one night sayin' stuff it, I'm a person, I can try this once to see if I'm still an addict. So I tried it just the once to see if I was still an addict . . . I was conning myself 'cos I'll always be an addict, I always have been an addict, and I think I knew when I took ma first hit of the heroin that I was conning myself. I was an addict wantin' to be stoned and I was looking for an excuse. And I tell you it was a hell of an excuse. I was stoned for a week and it was great.
>
> *(Jimmy)*

> If you go out and you go to where other junkies are goin' to be then you can say to yourself that I'm goin' there 'cos I want to see so-an'-so but all you really want to see is heroin and you want to get a bit of heroin and you want to use a bit of heroin. That's really the bottom line. But you tell yourself you'll go and see someone or go and see this or go and do that just to get near heroin. Maybe sometimes just to test yourself. But once you're there, deep in your mind, I think personally it is that you just want more heroin.
>
> *(Graham)*

On the basis of our data, it is not possible to determine the extent to which re-exposure to drugs was part of an attempt to reinforce the individual's abstinence or merely an excuse to use drugs again. It is, of course, also entirely possible that different people had genuinely different intentions.

Explaining relapse

Most of the reasons why former addicts return to the use of illegal drugs have been discussed, either directly or by implication, in the preceding pages. Basically, relapse occurs when the strategies which recovering addicts adopt to maintain their abstinence from drugs fail. In particular, it is vitally important that they avoid people who use drugs, establish a set of non-drug-related activities and relationships and develop a new, positive sense of self. For example, as we saw, associating with former friends and acquaintances or re-establishing contact with the drug-using world could rapidly seduce the recovering addict into using drugs again. It is also extremely important that the recovering addict finds constructive and satisfying ways of occupying his or her time. The loneliness, isolation and boredom associated with an inadequate drug-free life can all too easily make drugs appear attractive in comparison, and having nothing positive with which to replace the drug-taking lifestyle can prove fatal to attempts at recovery.

A lack of progress, then, in building a rewarding life away from drugs can play a major part in re-addiction. Similarly, if the new life that a recovering addict has established, with its new activities and relationships, is seriously threatened or damaged, the individual's resolve can be severely undermined and the temptation to re-enter the world of drugs can become irresistible. Prominent among these events are the loss of a job or the ending of a relationship. Personal crises, emotional traumas and the emergence of serious problems could also precipitate a return to drugs. According to some of our sample, the risk of relapse was increased when they were feeling emotionally fragile or hurt: at such times drugs might re-emerge as their established way of coping with such difficulties.

> If I'm hurt about somethin', if things are difficult for me to deal with emotionally, that's when I'm in danger, that's when I'm most at risk of using.
>
> *(Angela)*

It is important to emphasise, though, that many recovering addicts are perfectly capable of withstanding difficulties in their lives. This was certainly true of the majority of our sample. Most of them did not simply crumble at the first sign of adversity. On the contrary, the majority of the recovering addicts we interviewed were able to establish new lives and identities that were sufficiently robust to deal with a range of problems and even with major threats to the stability of their new lives. A key factor in their ability to cope with such difficulties and to resist temptation was their reason for stopping. As we saw earlier, giving up drugs in order to change one's life and repair a spoiled identity was a much more powerful and compelling motivation than doing it for more utilitarian reasons. It was those who were motivated by the latter who were most likely to experience difficulty in dealing with the exigencies of life and with threats to their stability. The picture we wish to present, then, is optimistic rather than pessimistic. While relapse is a very real and ever-present danger for the recovering addict, our sample provide ample testimony to the fact that it is certainly not inevitable and that strategies for preventing it can be highly effective.

While this chapter has been largely concerned with the recovering addicts' own efforts to stay off drugs, the following chapter considers their views on the part that drug services played in their recovery.

6 The addicts' views of drug services

In seeking to understand the process through which individuals are able to overcome their dependence upon illegal drugs, it is important to look at their experience of those services that have been provided to help them in that endeavour. Over the last 10 to 15 years there has been a major growth in consumerism within the health and social services and it is now commonplace for these services to obtain the views of their clients and to include these in service planning. Despite this, there have been relatively few attempts to obtain drug users' views of the services provided to them. In this chapter we look at our recovering addicts' views and experiences of the services with which they had been in contact.

Perhaps the first thing to say here is that, with the exception of methadone, about which many of our recovering addicts spoke at considerable length, it was notable how little time our interviewees spent talking about the contribution of drug-misuse services when describing their recovery. The impression one had from listening to their accounts was that, while the various drug-misuse services they had been in contact with had made a contribution to their eventual recovery, that contribution was more peripheral than central. For the majority of our interviewees their eventual recovery was presented more in terms of a personal challenge they had faced and overcome, rather than in terms of the contribution of specific services. This may come as rather unwelcome news to those working within drug-misuse services in Scotland and elsewhere. However, it is important to underline the fact that, simply because our interviewees described their recovery more in terms of their own efforts and challenges than in terms of the contribution of drug-misuse services, this does not mean that those services played a minimal role in their recovery. It may simply have been that their own efforts at coming off and staying off appeared more salient to the individuals than the range of services provided to assist them in their recovery.

We have chosen to begin our discussion by looking first at the recovering addicts' views of methadone for the simple reason that they had much more to say about methadone than about any other area of drug-service provision.

Methadone: life saver or life sentence?

Methadone is a heroin substitute that is widely used within the UK and elsewhere for the treatment of individuals addicted to opiate drugs. Methadone is generally made available to drug misusers in terms of one of two prescribing regimes. First, the drug can be prescribed on a reducing basis. Within this regime a doctor agrees to provide decreasing amounts of methadone to the addict over a specified period. The length of this period may be determined jointly by the doctor and the addict or it may be determined solely by the doctor. The second basis upon which methadone may be prescribed is in terms of a maintenance regime. Here there is little or no expectation that the individual will reduce his or her dose of methadone in the short to medium term and the individual may be prescribed methadone over many years. In the first scenario the principal concern of the prescribing physician may be to avoid the individual becoming addicted to methadone itself while in the second scenario the concern may be to foster a level of stability within the individual's life over many years in the hope that, in time, he or she may be able to address the basis for his or her addiction and begin the road to recovery.

There is probably no area of drug-misuse service provision that is more controversial than methadone. For some people methadone is an extraordinarily valuable drug that can be of great assistance to individuals addicted to heroin. For others, prescribing methadone to a heroin addict is akin to prescribing alcohol to an alcoholic. In this context, it may be helpful to briefly review some of the research in this area before looking at what our recovering addicts had to say about their own experiences of methadone.

Despite the controversy that surrounds its use, the evidence from research indicates that methadone can make a very positive contribution in reducing drug users' risk behaviour and assisting their recovery from addiction. For example, research has shown that methadone-maintained addicts commit fewer crimes than their non-methadone-maintained counterparts. In a study of 617 patients enrolled on a methadone-maintenance programme, Ball and Ross (1991) identified a 79 per cent reduction in the number of offences committed between the year before admission and the most recent year in methadone maintenance. In a study by Lehmann *et al.* (1993), after one year on methadone mainten-ance 89 per cent of 51 patients had no contact with the judicial system compared to 58 per cent of addicts on entry. Methadone maintenance has also been shown to be associated with lower levels of HIV-related risk behaviour. Longshore and colleagues compared 105 patients on methadone maintenance with 153 patients who were not on a method-one programme. The rate of needle sharing in the last year amongst the methadone group was 63 per cent compared to 79 per cent in the non-methadone group (Longshore *et al.* 1993). Methadone maintenance has also been shown to be associated with a reduced risk of overdose amongst opiate addicts. In a two-year randomised study undertaken by Gunne and Gronbladh (1981) there were no deaths in the methadone-maintenance group (n = 17) and two deaths in the no-treatment group (n = 17). Bell and colleagues (1992) have reported that patients who apply to, but are rejected for, methadone maintenance have a higher mortality rate than addicts who are treated on such a programme. There also appear to be benefits associated with methadone in terms of reten-tion in treatment, with addicts who are receiving methadone remaining in contact with treatment services for longer than those of their peers not receiving methadone (Ball and Ross 1991). Within the UK, the largest single study assessing the impact of drug-misuse treatment is the National Treatment Outcome Research Study (NTORS). This project involves regular assessment of a cohort of drug misusers who started drug-misuse treatment in 1995. Included within the NTORS study are both methadone-maintenance and methadone-reduction programmes. Amongst those individuals recruited into methadone-maintenance pro-grammes, 57.4 per cent had used heroin in the previous three months, while one year after starting treatment this had fallen to 24 per cent. For those addicts recruited into the methadone-reduction programmes heroin use had reduced from a high of 70.2 per cent at intake to 30.4 per cent at one-year follow-up (Gossop *et al.* 2000).

Despite extensive research into the efficacy of methadone, there are two areas in which our understanding of its role and contribution is relatively undeveloped. First, we know very little about the long-term impact of methadone on the length of a drug-using career. Put simply, the question here is: do individuals remain addicts longer as a result of being prescribed methadone over many years than they would have done had they not been prescribed the drug? Second, we know very little about drug users' own views of methadone. One of the few studies that has reported on this was carried out by Neale who interviewed 80 addicts receiving methadone in Scotland (Neale 1998, 1999a, 1999b). According to Neale, the addicts interviewed in her study regarded methadone as a 'complex drug', perceiving it as having both positive and negative consequences. Only 12 of the addicts interviewed in her research felt that methadone had no detrimental effects. In terms of the main positive benefits, around half of the addicts interviewed said that, in their view, their emotional and physical health had been improved as a result of being prescribed methadone, more than a third said that methadone had helped reduce their use of illicit drugs and a quarter of the interviewees said that methadone had reduced their participation in crime. Some referred to the financial benefits which had accrued to them as a result of not having to spend large sums of money on illicit drugs and others said that it had improved their family relationships. With regard to the negative consequences of methadone, nearly two-thirds of the addicts interviewed in Neale's study commented that they had experienced negative health effects resulting from their use of the drug. These included: constipation, sweating, sleeping problems, tiredness, stiffness and hallucinations. Over half of the addicts said that methadone had caused similar, and in some cases greater, problems for them than the heroin which they had been using previously. Other individuals commented that the dosage of methadone they had been given had been reduced too soon or that they had been given insufficient amounts of methadone in the first place. As we show in the remainder of this chapter, many of the individuals interviewed in our own research echoed the views of those interviewed by Neale.

Around half (36) of the recovering addicts in our study had personal experience of having been prescribed methadone. For some of these individuals methadone was seen as a wonder drug that had saved them from the depths of their addiction. The main benefit of methadone, as they saw it, was the opportunity it provided for creating a period of stability in an otherwise chaotic lifestyle. Importantly, by providing a methadone prescription, the unpleasant effects of drug withdrawal could be reduced or removed.

It just takes your sore bellies away, you don't get stoned the way you do with smack. If you take a bit of methadone you don't get stoned off it. It just straightens you up so you're not vomiting, you're not sick, you've not got diarrhoea and sore bones. It just takes all them away from you.

(Jane)

However, the stability that was associated with a regular methadone pre-scription went far beyond the avoidance of the unpleasant effects of drug withdrawal. Receiving a regular, legal supply of methadone also meant that individuals no longer had to devote each day to searching for black market drugs or engaging in the criminal activity necessary to support their drug purchases.

It saved [me] from having to get up every day and having to get money and go about finding drugs. It's torture. I'm glad I've got a doctor, I should have gone to the doctor earlier.

(Andy)

I've been all right for four or five years since I've been prescribed the methadone. No trouble, back to normal with the family. If they hadn't prescribed it, I would probably be in the jail doing five or ten years . . . I'd have done an armed robbery. If I didn't have the prescription, I don't know where I'd be now . . . it makes a big difference because you don't have to go out and steal or beg or sell yourself or whatever.

(Joyce)

Crucially, being on methadone facilitated the development of a new life for some addicts and made a future without drugs appear attainable. For Claire and Alison it meant being able to pursue a more 'normal' lifestyle.

Yea, I'm quite stable now with what I'm on. I'm trying to get a house, I've got my life back, well not the way I would like it, but I'm getting there compared to what I used to be. I think the methadone has really helped me do that. If I never had my methadone I wouldn't be like this now. I'd still be using drugs and not bothering about getting a house or anything like that. Because I was taking drugs every day I was having to go out and get money but when you're on a methadone script you don't have to do that. It's there for you, you've got no worries, you know you can get on with everyday life knowing that your medication's there for you. You're not going to be rattling, know what I mean?

(Claire)

I'd say my life is a lot better now. I mean, I like being able to go out and buy things and not just buy drugs with every single penny I have. Like I'm trying to save now for Christmas 'cos like for my kids' first Christmas . . . I never had any money so I ordered hundreds of things out of this catalogue and then I was getting chased up for it and that. But last year was really the first Christmas that I've had money and I've been able to go out and buy and that.

(Alison)

For Lizzie it meant also being able to regain some measure of self-esteem.

When I was usin', I was just going out during the day to shoplift. Every moment my eyes were open I would have to say, 'Have I got money?' It's just a completely different lifestyle . . . And you start to get a feelin' of self-worth. Being normal again is the best thing.

(Lizzie)

Methadone also helped others to begin to rebuild relationships that had been damaged by many years of drug use.

I didn't want to be this bastard, this person that was really getting very nasty if I couldn't get it. I don't mean violently nasty toward my kids . . . Just sitting staring at the TV, not talking to anyone. I knew I had to do something, I had to think about my kids, my wife, my life for instance. I mean, what was I going to end up with? Nothing. If I had lost her, the kids, what would I have been left with? 50 mls of methadone a day, that's what I would have been left with . . . Because I was getting worse and worse, we were on the slope. I went to the doctor, I knew myself this is it, I can do something now I can stop spending money on drugs. That is the first thing when you get a prescription from the doctor. There's a lot of folk who get a prescription and they still buy drugs. That's their problem. For me the first reason I made a move to the doctor was to stop spending all my money you know. After that I said to myself, 'This is great I've got my money back, I'm getting a bit of my life back again.'

(Bill)

Having a legal drug supply also strengthened the individual's capacity to break relationships with drug-using contacts. As we saw in the previous chapter, this was an important element in the process of staying off drugs.

[With] a methadone script I'll not be going near them people that are doing a lot of stuff. I make a point of staying well clear of them 'cos that's not the life that I want.

(Debbie)

I didn't have to deal with any of the nitty gritty back street, black market any more . . . you're sort of pulling out of the culture slowly, comin' out of the black market culture.

(Kate)

Methadone was also regarded positively by some of our recovering addicts because it had helped them to reduce their drug-related risk behaviour, most notably with regard to reducing or removing the need to inject.

The only problem I noticed was that if I didn't do something about it I'd be injecting it every day. So I got a prescription for methadone, which meant I wasn't injecting every day. All the guys I went about with were into injecting Temgesic, they were still doing it, but I never did, 'cos I was taking methadone and I would rather die than inject Temgesic.

(Charlie)

In talking about their use of methadone many of the recovering addicts drew a distinction between the euphoric effects associated with black market drugs and the more therapeutic effects of methadone. It was important in their own eyes, and in the eyes of others, for methadone to be seen not as just one more drug to which they were addicted but as part of the solution to their problem.

For me, my methadone just makes me feel like what you do. Just lets me get up and get about.

(Sally)

Some people say the more methadone you get the better the gouch [drug-induced stupor], but I'm not interested in the gouch. I'm just interested in taking the methadone every day to help me get on with my life, to help me get back to my old self to try to get back to work.

(Rhona)

I don't take methadone now for the stone, I take it because I need it to feel normal like the way you feel normal, get up in the morning, you feel normal. For me to feel the way you feel I need my 30 mls of methadone a day.

(Kathleen)

However, not all of our interviewees viewed methadone in this way and it was clear that some individuals were attracted to methadone because it produced a similar effect to the heroin they had been using for many years:

I [saw] a drug counsellor on the Friday and he said how much heroin are you using and I told him a gram a day. He said how much have you had today and I said only a tenner [£10] bag. He said OK I'll start you off with 50 mls of methadone and I [thought] OK. I [asked] my wee brother after he left, 'Will that get me stoned?' That was all that was in my head. I wanted to come off but I still wanted that feeling and my brother says honestly Judy that'll get you through. I said right. So I went and got it and I was like, 'What do you do with this?' I thought you injected it but you swallow it. It doesn't hit you for about an hour after you've taken it. I spewed everywhere, absolutely sick absolutely ill. But that was only one day then I felt really good and I got stoned. I got stoned for months and months. I took 50 mls every single day.

(Judy)

For many of the individuals interviewed in our research methadone had been of enormous benefit. If it had not always actually helped them to come off drugs, it had at least afforded them a period of stability within which they had been able to begin to consider the possibility of recovery. However, although it clearly helped some addicts to recover from their addiction, others believed that methadone had had a detrimental effect on their lives. The most commonly expressed criticism of the drug had to do with its perceived addictiveness. For example, some of our interviewees claimed that coming off methadone was more difficult than coming off heroin.

> I never knew it was going to be so hard to come off. It's harder to come off than heroin. It kills you. My boyfriend calls it the government's poison. 'That's no' helping people, that's the government's poison,' he says. He really doesn't want to go on it 'cos he goes to the jail a lot and he's seen people and what they go through and he says he can't do that. He says a lot of people commit suicide because they can't handle it in jail because of the methadone withdrawal.
>
> *(Sharon)*

> See methadone, they're givin' out a terrible message with that. They're tellin' people it's a cure but it's not. It just prolongs the illness, that's all it does. It's more addictive than heroin. I had more problems comin' off methadone than I did with heroin.
>
> *(Douglas)*

Although there were those for whom the regularity of a legal drug supply had enabled them to create an element of stability in their lives there were others who claimed that methadone had undermined their ability to function at an everyday level because they found themselves in a perpetual 'daze'. For example, Catriona described being totally disorientated by the drug and being unable to function normally.

> I didn't know where I was or nothing, I was just constantly in a daze. I was going down to the chemist to pick up my methadone and I couldn't remember getting it. I'd been down an hour later and arguing with them 'Where's my methadone?' Silly things like that. And I was forgetting where the child was and just really away with it.
>
> *(Catriona)*

Some of those in our study commented bitterly that when methadone had first been prescribed to them nobody had explained how addictive the drug could be.

> I didn't see a day when I didn't have it [methadone]. I suppose I thought I was going to be stabilised for life. But then when I came up here and tried to do a detox to come off it, it was only then I realised how bad it was. These doctors will give you a methadone script but none of them will tell you that if you decide to come off it this is going to happen or that is going to happen.
>
> *(Dorothy)*

The resentment which some individuals felt at not having the addictiveness of methadone fully explained to them was part of a wider dissatisfaction with the way in which methadone was made available. In particular, a number of our interviewees took the view that writing out a prescription for methadone was an easy option for individual doctors unwilling to spend the time necessary to address the root causes of their drug addiction.

> I'm really annoyed at the doctors for giving me methadone prescriptions 'cos it's like doctors don't want to get to the root of the drug problems. I'm not blaming the doctors in any way but it's like instead of just giving people methadone scripts to get them off their back or whatever, they should sit and talk to them and ask them why they take drugs, what made them take drugs and things like that.
>
> *(Maria)*

Some even claimed that they had been forced against their wishes to start on a methadone prescription.

> Then I went to my doctor and got prescribed dihydrocodeine to start with and he cut us off them, I asked for Temgesic, he put us on the Temgesic then he put us on the methadone but I didn't want on the methadone. I've seen too many people die from methadone so I said I don't want the methadone and I kept refusing and refusing so he struck us off. I was off for a couple of weeks and I went back to him and he says do you want on the

methadone. So I was forced into taking methadone more or less, it was like he wasn't giving us an option.

(Steve)

A small number (six) of our interviewees commented that as a result of being too ready to prescribe methadone, their doctor had, in effect, become their drug dealer:

I mean it wasn't his fault, I mean as a junkie addicted now to methadone he was my dealer, you know. If he's going to keep handing it out I'm going to keep taking it, you know what I mean?

(Kate)

I was two years on the methadone . . . and to me my doctor was my drug dealer.

(Laura)

However, while going on methadone at all seemed to be problematic for some of our sample, the length of time for which they remained on it and the amount of the drug they were prescribed appeared to be a source of concern for an even higher proportion of them. Some of them volunteered that, in their view, they had been kept on methadone for too long while others felt that the level of methadone they had been on was too high.

Because 50 mls was just too much for me I was starting to gouch with it and I didn't want to. I wanted to be on my medication to help me, I didn't want to be gouching and not know what's going on around me. It's no good walking about and not knowing what's going on. You're better being wide awake seeing reality, let it hit you in the face. I don't understand how these doctors give folk 90 mls 'cos they're sending them to sleep. They're just getting as much out of it as if they were using drugs. I think some doctors are just giving it to get rid of them, they don't want to waste time . . . I'm a little bit biased with people that take too much 'cos I think the doctors are just feeding them and making their head bloated and they're just walking about the same as they were when they were on drugs. They're no' really helping them much, just helping them feed their habit with giving them that much methadone.

(Brenda)

Some of our interviewees were especially critical of the policy of maintenance prescribing whereby addicts are kept on methadone as a way of stabilising their lives but where little attempt is made to end their reliance upon it. A third of the drug users in our study who had been prescribed methadone volunteered the view that a policy of gradually reducing the amount of methadone that is prescribed was preferable to simple maintenance since the former offers the prospect of coming off the drug while the latter does not. To put it another way, while prescribed reduction was seen as being a form of treatment, prescribed maintenance was often regarded as an alternative form of addiction.

They [doctors] just want to leave you on [methadone] and then you're no' shopliftin' and you're no' buying drugs and you're no' keeping the percentages of crime rate up. 'There's your prescription and away you go till I see the next person.'

(Chrissy)

Prescribed reduction, gradual reduction is, I would say, the best way to do it . . . To me, I had a drug addiction when I was gettin' it every week from the doctor, just script after script. To me that was just a habit . . . And a habit's a habit, it doesn't matter what it is.

(Martin)

It [methadone] was supposed to help people come off drugs but now everybody is just gettin' it for the sake of gettin' it and they're not comin' off drugs. People I know have been on it for fifteen years. It's a lifetime.

(Barbara)

However, according to a small number of our recovering addicts, getting their methadone prescription altered in the direction of reducing or removing it could be difficult. Three of our interviewees reported that, even where they had raised with drug agency staff the possibility that they should reduce their methadone intake or even stop it altogether, such requests were not always listened to sympathetically.

The only thing I didn't like was I didn't like being on for so long. It was too long. I was on it for eighteen months and I could have been on it for a lot longer. When you go into [name of drug project] and you are getting interviewed, they don't ask how long you want to be on methadone for. Whereas for some people it's good for years, for others it's not. They didn't ask me how long I wanted to be on it for. I was there from September to February and I went back to my doctor and he kept prescribing it. When I went to the clinic in August, I was like, what about when I come off it and she said oh don't worry about it, you can start on your 50 when you come back.

(Rhona)

On the other hand, it was precisely the prospect of having their methadone dose reduced or removed that caused anxiety for others in our study. For those who had become addicted to methadone, the prospect of being taken off it or of having their dose reduced was highly problematic and, according to their own accounts, could make them extremely anxious. The extent of that anxiety is very evident in the following extract from the interview with Judy.

I got through Christmas and I was still shoplifting and had loads and loads of money. So they started reducing my methadone and it was fine until I got down to 30 mls and I started going, 'I can't handle this, you're going too quick.' I wasn't getting that stoned feeling that was getting me through every day. So I started to panic. I wasn't withdrawing 'cos it took my withdrawals away, I never felt any withdrawals, but I wasn't getting that stoned feeling in my brain so I started panicking. I [said] to them 'Don't reduce me I can't just do it just leave me there now . . .' But she was adamant . . . she was a right bitch. She didn't listen to me and just said, 'I'm taking you right off the methadone.'

(Judy)

Finally, many of the recovering addicts interviewed in our research referred to a range of unpleasant side-effects associated with methadone. This included claims that methadone could cause extreme constipation, excessive sweating and, even, that it could 'rot your bones'.

The methadone, that kind of stabilised me [though] I hated going for it and hated taking it. I used to call it jungle juice . . . I done a

lot of research on methadone. I knew it ate away at your bone
marrow after years and years of using it and that put me off. That
was in my head from the first day I took it. I thought fuck this is
going to end up in a wheelchair.

(Lorna)

Methadone was OK, taking it was a pain in the backside 'cos it
makes you constipated. It makes you sweat, the sweat was worse,
it was horrible you could feel it on your skin sweating . . . but it
made you feel brilliant, as in terms of your addiction. I mean you
could stop taking drugs, take methadone and feel brilliant, great.
So that was a relief. When you consider the sweats, all I had to do
was to make sure that I didn't want to go anywhere. Stay in the
house but I didn't really want to go out anyway and face anyone.

(Douglas)

While these side-effects did not entirely negate our interviewees'
appreciation of the part that methadone played in helping them to come
off illegal drugs, they did mean that, for many of them, the experience of
being on methadone was not a pleasant one.

To sum up, it is clear that methadone had been of enormous benefit to
many of the recovering addicts in our study. For those individuals,
methadone had provided the opportunity to begin the process of extric-
ating themselves from a drug-using lifestyle and had enabled them to
create a level of stability in their lives from which they could begin to
regain a sense of their own self-worth and to rebuild relationships with
other people. By having a regular prescribed supply of an opiate substitute, the individual no longer had to experience the daily effects of
drug withdrawal, nor embark on the daily hunt for drugs on the black
market, nor involve themselves in the many illegal activities that had
previously been necessary to support their drug habit. It had also enabled
some individuals to break their contacts with other drug users; something that, as we saw in Chapter 5, was central to successful recovery.
There were, then, clear winners out of the methadone regime. Equally,
however, there were clear losers as well; these included individuals who,
in one way or another, felt that their drug use had been made worse – or
certainly no better – as a result of the methadone which had been
prescribed to them. For these individuals methadone had simply become
another drug to which they were addicted. Many of them feared the
effects of methadone withdrawal and, alongside that, the possibility that

they might be required to reduce their methadone consumption. They were critical of the ease with which methadone was being provided and the lack of clear information as to the addictiveness of the drug itself. They also resented the fact that, on at least some occasions, writing out a prescription for methadone had been the easy option for doctors who, they said, were unwilling to address the real causes of their drug addiction.

From the accounts of the recovering addicts in our study, it is clear that methadone could have both positive and negative outcomes for the individual. As a result, we believe there is a need to continually assess the suitability of methadone for each of the individuals to whom it is provided. There will be some who will require to be on methadone for many years. Equally, however, there will be others who will have ceased to derive any therapeutic benefit from the drug and for whom it may well be more appropriate to cease or reduce its use.

We now consider what our interviewees had to say about the other services with which they had been in contact.

Counselling and support

Many of the individuals in our study expressed their deep appreciation of the various counsellors and support groups to whom they had been able to go for help or to talk about their needs. Sometimes, what they required was to have their resolve reinforced by someone else while, on other occasions, they needed reassurance that the temptations they were experiencing were normal and that they could conquer them and succeed. They particularly needed somebody to talk to when things got difficult and they were tempted to use drugs again. For instance, Bridie was in no doubt that being part of a support group had played a significant part in her recovery.

> It's like sometimes I can't come up with all the answers myself and I have to say to somebody, 'Look, I want to get stoned out o' ma head, I need help here.' I can do that in the team. If I couldn't do it in the team I'd make sure I had somebody I could do that with to keep me straight.
>
> *(Bridie)*

On the whole, the views expressed by our interviewees regarding the value of such counselling were positive and it seemed that many members of our sample had accepted that important progress could be made in addressing their needs through the process of talking about various aspects of their lives with a counsellor. Frequently, the recovering addicts needed to exorcise certain demons associated with their addiction by discussing with sympathetic others what had led to them getting into drugs in the first place and the profound sense of guilt, remorse and disgust that they felt towards the life they had led. In short, there was a lot of emotional baggage to work through and to resolve and it was here that formal counselling could be of particular value. Harry, who did not receive any formal counselling while recovering from his addiction, had no doubt that it would have helped him considerably to have had someone to talk to about the problems which he had in maintaining abstinence.

> Right, after the physical is the mental. Just learning to cope again. I didn't have much help and I still did it but it would've been a lot easier with help. I don't even mean residential, like going to a place to get dried out. Just maybe speaking to a counsellor now and again would be a big help and just sort of, I mean, you've got to deal with your emotions as well. You've got to learn to do that and it can be quite difficult.
>
> *(Harry)*

Various drug projects and self-help groups were also reported as playing a vital role in the healing process. One of the most prominent of these groups was Narcotics Anonymous (NA) whose activities were especially valued by members of our sample.

> NA is a great support for me. I'm not wanting to get addicted to NA or anything like that, but that's where I go for help. I couldn't do it myself. I'd maybe go and visit a straight pal or go for a walk or something. If that still didn't help, I'd go and see if I could get in contact wi' somebody from NA. Maybe hearing them say, 'I've felt like that myself before', or, 'Take it one day at a time, if you look too far ahead you'll end up cracking'. It's a hard battle.
>
> *(Susie)*

But for me, I was fortunate because I'd made a lot o' friends in Narcotics Anonymous, people that had been where I'd been and knew what I was goin' through. So I had a lot of help and support, which I think is very important 'cos you need to talk. You can't keep it to yourself, it's much too dangerous for us.

(Dorothy)

The ability to drop into a facility without a prior arrangement, or to contact someone on the telephone day or night, was especially valued by our respondents since challenges to their attempts to remain abstinent could occur at any time and certainly did not respect conventional schedules.

I do get cravings quite a lot. I go to NA meetings a lot. They're really friendly and helpful. Any support I need, they'll give it to me straight away. Any problems, I just need to pick up the phone. And I really do appreciate it.

(Tom)

Many of our interviewees also commented positively on the opportunity to meet with other drug users who were similarly seeking to come off drugs or who had succeeded in doing so.

When I used to go in the drop-in centre in London you weren't really talking about drugs, you were talking about what was on telly or whatever, which was entirely different, you weren't talking drugs just normal chat. When there was somewhere to go to it sort of motivated you a wee bit especially in the coming off process, I think you need somewhere to feel comfortable. I think you need somewhere to learn how to sort of start to build your confidence.

(Mary)

I eventually posted the application [for NA] and they took me quite quick. I was in within the week or something. And then when I went in there it was like all these people talking about the feelings that I had for so many years and it was like total relief. Away from all the madness and all that it allowed me to talk about my feelings. And also writing, we did a lot of writing about what I'd done to get drugs. Being able to see it for what it really is. And I think the biggest relief I got was I knew my feelings wouldn't kill me. These people had feelings of self-obsession, especially addicts and that there's a programme to overcome that,

that we don't need to be so self-obsessed, we can turn that around to helping other people and not being self-centred all the time.

(Barbara)

The importance of being able to talk to others about the stresses and strains involved in trying to come off drugs and in resisting the various temptations to resume using them is evident in the extract below.

There is quite a few stressful situations which I'm having to deal with. But as long as I talk about them I feel OK. If I just keep them bottled up to myself I know what will happen, I'll just lead myself back to drugs.

(Tom)

Based on the accounts of our interviewees, there appeared to be three main advantages to being able to talk to other recovering addicts, whether the latter were employed as counsellors or were simply fellow members of a self-help group. First, they understood, first hand, what the recovering addicts were going through and were able to relate to their struggle and to empathise with them. Second, they had credibility; they had been there themselves and they knew what they were talking about. As a result, their advice and guidance carried particular weight among the members of our sample. Third, the example provided by other addicts who had successfully overcome their addiction gave inspiration to those who were not so far along the road and helped to sustain the hope that they too could succeed. Jane described the encouragement she received from former addicts as follows:

Some of these people are ex-addicts. It gives you something to aim for too. You're lookin' at them and sayin', 'Well, if that's where they are now, surely I can be there in a couple of years or however long it's goin' to take.' They're givin' you a wee bit of hope that there is people who can do it and get their lives together so that gives you a wee bit more to hope for.

(Jane)

On the basis of their own personal experience of having been counselled, a number of the recovering addicts felt that they had a unique contribution to make in helping other addicts come off drugs. Some of them were actively seeking voluntary or paid work that would allow them to provide such assistance:

I help other addicts. That is the most important thing for me is to help other addicts. I attend a woman's meeting on a Monday night, a Narcotics Anonymous meeting. It's quite hard for women to get clean, I feel as if it's a bit harder for women than it is for men. There's a lot of shame and different stuff that they can't speak about. We go there every week, open that up and I'm constantly all the time helping addicts and doing that and going to the meetings. Just living my life, know what I mean, just doing the simple things that I was never able to do before.

(Dorothy)

Finally, the various counselling services that they attended also assisted the recovering addicts in another important respect. Specifically, they helped them to occupy their time and to fill the void that was left when they gave up drugs.

Detoxification and rehabilitation

The importance of detoxification and rehabilitation services was emphasised repeatedly by our interviewees. For many individuals, detoxification was a very important part of the process of coming off drugs. A number of our interviewees also spoke about the value of being able to attend detoxification services that were physically distant from the areas in which they had pursued their addict lifestyle and where they were likely to meet other drug-using associates:

I think the best thing would be to go to a detox where I'm actually out of the place, I'm actually in a different environment, I'm not in a place where I could just get drugs when I want them. I'm in a closed environment and they could treat us like, cut us down gradually and eventually get off it and eventually go to a rehabilitation centre to get them to help us deal with going back to the outside world but without drugs.

(Sally)

The importance of helping addicts to re-integrate back into society was also underlined by a number of our interviewees. There was a feeling, though, that many of the services provided to assist addicts tended to be concentrated at the early stages of their recovery and that once they were off drugs there were few services available to help them to rehabilitate back into society:

> I'm the only person that's stayed clean and it hasn't done me any justice. I'd be as well using 'cos the people I know that's been clean right, when they have gone back to using that has opened doors for them, there are people saying this lassie needs help, she's got kids or he needs help. What happens though to the people that are clean and that have been through all that? Where's the support and back-up for them? It isn't there, it doesn't exist. You maybe get one or two that'll come up and spend a few hours chatting to you but these couple of hours dwindle away until they don't want to come and chat to you 'cos you're not a problem any more, you've no' got problems, you're no' taking drugs. Your problems are everyday problems that everybody else has got to cope with so you're no different from anybody else, that is how it's seen.
>
> *(Bridie)*

Clearly there is a problem if, as Bridie's experience would seem to suggest, there is a notable decrease in the involvement of drug services once the individual has made progress in overcoming his or her addiction. It would plainly be a tragedy if, in the face of such an experience, the individual came to the conclusion that there were more people interested in helping them when they were an addict than when they had ceased their drug use and, as a result, began to question the value of the progress they had made in overcoming their addiction.

Conclusion

The recovering addicts in our study demonstrated that they were perfectly capable of reflecting on the range of services provided to them and of formulating a view as to which of those services had assisted them in their efforts to come off drugs. They were also perfectly capable of identifying those aspects of current service provision that had made the task of recovery more difficult than perhaps it needed to be. Recovering addicts have much to say that is of value about drug services and we believe it is important that their views are listened to and integrated into service provision. In the concluding chapter we look in greater detail at the implications of our research for the various services provided to assist individuals recovering from dependent drug use. However, we would like to make one point here. It is a point that many might regard as being so obvious as not to require stating but it is so fundamental to the provision of services that we feel it is worth introducing here. Different people will be attracted to different services and will derive different benefits from those services at different times. We need to ensure that there is as close a match as possible between what people want from the services provided for them and what they are able to get from these services. We also need to avoid the situation in which a narrow range of services is provided on a routine basis without regard to individual needs. Finally, we need to ensure that our drug services are sufficiently flexible to respond to the shifting needs of individuals over time.

7 Conclusion

In this the final chapter we begin by tying together the various elements of recovery from drug addiction that we have explored in this book. We then discuss a number of salient methodological issues before going on to conclude by considering what we believe to be the main implications of our research for drug-misuse services.

Recovery from addiction

We have sought in this book to show how a successful decision to stop using drugs can be seen as part of an attempt by the addict to manage the extreme discomfort of a badly spoiled identity. It appears from our study that at the heart of most successful decisions to exit drug misuse is the recognition by individuals that their identities have been seriously damaged by their addiction and the lifestyle that accompanies it. This, in turn, stimulates a desire to restore their identities and to establish a different kind of future for themselves. It seems that it is when addicts recognise the extent to which their 'self' has been degraded, and resolve to change for that reason, that successful and enduring recovery is most likely to occur. In this context, considerations of the present and of the future are inseparable. As Biernacki has put it, '... identity not only encompasses the past in a biographical sense but contains a sense of the future (what people hope to be or what they fear becoming) ...' (1986, p. 21).

Our analysis of the role of identity in the recovery from dependent drug use corresponds closely with the work of Biernacki and his colleagues. Although Biernacki's study was concerned exclusively with the process of 'natural', or unaided, recovery from addiction, we believe that the same psycho-social processes are in operation in relation to most recovering addicts. For Biernacki (1986), the key to the recovery process lies in the realisation by addicts that their damaged sense of self has to be restored together with a reawakening of their old identities and/or the establishment of new ones. Similarly, our findings parallel Shaffer and Jones's (1989) depiction of the addict's identity crisis as an 'epistemologic shift'. This psychological reorientation is described by them as constituting a major re-evaluation by the addict of his or her life and the place of drugs in it. According to Shaffer and Jones, this process is 'Often experienced as a life crisis, the addict recognises that his or her lifestyle must change if he or she is to regain control' (Shaffer and Jones 1989, p. 153). Importantly, from this moment on, problems are no longer perceived by users as being the result of external events but, rather, the result of their own actions, and can therefore be changed.

Two things seem to be required for a successful decision to stop using illegal drugs: (1) a motivation to exit which is more powerful than the fear of stopping; and (2) a sense of a future that is potentially different from the present. The identity crisis that addicts experience provides both. The essence of this crisis is a serious conflict between what the addicts have become on the one hand and, on the other hand, what they feel they should be and what they would like to be. This crisis in their sense of self can include disgust at their present lifestyle, distress at what they are doing to loved ones, fear of serious illness or even death or, indeed, a combination of these and other factors. For many addicts there comes a turning point at which they review critically what they have become, do not like what they see and decide to change. Prins describes this moment as follows: '. . . eventually there comes a phase in the trajectory in which the addict has tried to come to terms with the trajectory, a point where he decided that he did not want to go on in the same manner, that something really had to change . . . They knew that it had to stop. The price was too high to leave things alone and go on as in the past' (1994, p. 92).

This turning point comes when an accumulation of experiences and events gradually reveals to the addict the depths to which he or she has sunk and, at the same time, provides a vision of an alternative future. As we saw, the effect of these experiences is indirect and is mediated by the way in which the addict interprets their significance in relation to his or her sense of self. Many of these revelatory experiences and messages had, of course, been around for some time prior to the decision to stop. What is different when the decision to stop is made is the stage the user is at in his or her career and the way in which the implications of these inputs are interpreted in relation to the addict's sense of self. In short, the addict is ready for change. Frequently, this decisive moment is precipitated by a crisis or trigger of some sort, which acts to force the addict to confront the nature and extent of his or her spoiled identity. As we saw, the addict's former, or residual, identity played an important part in the process of identity review and self-realisation, as did periods of abstinence associated with failed attempts to stop. Both of these gave the users alternative views of themselves and of their possible future.

There is an important distinction to be made here between addicts feeling that they *should* stop and their *wanting* to stop. It was clear from our data that many addicts believed that they *should* stop for some time before eventually deciding to do so. For example, this could be for the sake of their health, for their families or their partners or to avoid prison. However, the evidence of our study is that they are only likely to succeed in stopping long term once they have decided that it is what they *want* to do. In addition, though, they have to want to do it for the right reasons. In his study of ex-addicts, Prins reports that, 'without a single exception, the people in the sample . . . said that, "If you want to get clean, you have to do it yourself."' (1994, pp. 36–7). Prins's interpretation of this is that 'what they really mean to say is that you must be *really* [his italics] serious when you want to get clean' (p. 36). While we would not dispute the importance of a serious intent in the attempt to give up drugs, we believe that the key to understanding the process is not so much that the addicts have to do it *by* themselves but that they have to do it *for* themselves. This was a common theme in our recovering addicts' accounts of their successful attempts to stop; you had to quit because you no longer wanted to be an addict, not for some other more utilitarian purpose. Some had stopped previously, often on several occasions, for reasons that did not have to do with renewing their identity. However, giving up for such reasons was, in the view of our interviewees, generally a recipe for relapse.

In common with Biernacki (1986), we distinguished two main types of decision to exit drug misuse: rational decisions and rock bottom decisions. For us the main distinguishing feature of the rock bottom decision is that it is associated with the addict feeling that he or she simply has to stop. There is no other viable option. To carry on is unthinkable. In the period leading up to this decision, addicts will frequently contemplate or even attempt suicide. The rational decision is different in that, with it, it is simply a matter of the addict having a powerful desire to exit based on the unacceptable nature of what he or she has become. The identities of those who reach rock bottom are more profoundly damaged than are those of the addicts who make a rational decision to stop. As a result, the latter are able to deal with their problems in an apparently more considered and less emotive fashion. However, the two types of decision are part of the same category of experience and involve the same biographical work on the part of the addict. What both types of decision have in common is a desire on the part of individuals to rebuild their identity and their future.

Consistent with the work of others (Waldorf 1983, Biernacki 1986, Stall and Biernacki 1986), we have argued that a central component of successful recovery from addiction is the development of a renewed sense of identity on the part of the former addict and the acceptance of that new identity by his or her significant others. An important advantage of this theoretical approach is that its emphasis on identity creation and renewal provides a conceptual focus for understanding the integrated nature of the various strategies which addicts employ, and the way in which these cohere around a central goal. As we saw, the recovering addict's new identity not only needs to be sustained by an appropriate set of activities and relationships, it also requires positive reinforcement in the form of experiences which demonstrate the benefits and advantages of being drug-free and make the former addict feel good about him or herself. It is when this new social world comes under threat, or begins to disintegrate, that it becomes difficult for recovering addicts to sustain their new identities and relapse becomes more likely.

The transition to non-addict status is not an easy one, involving as it does a major disruption to the individual's life. All of a sudden, the social networks, values, activities and relationships that had defined and structured the addict's life are removed and a potential void is created. As we saw, it is essential that this gap is filled in an appropriate and constructive manner if the individual is to stand any chance of success in sustaining his or her recovery. In addition, of course, a new non-addict identity also has to be constructed and sustained. None of this happens on its own. It all has to be managed by the addicts themselves and often at a time when they are not feeling particularly robust. That so many manage the transition successfully is a tribute to their determination and resilience and to the strength of their desire to change.

The main tasks which the recovering addict has to accomplish are, firstly, the transformation of his or her identity from user to non-user and, secondly, the maintenance of a drug-free lifestyle. These tasks are mutually dependent and a set of common strategies is applied to both. As we saw, the two main strategies through which the addicts sought to achieve their goals were (1) the avoidance of their former drug-using network and friends, and (2) the development of a set of non-drug-related activities and relationships. These were also the principal strategies identified by Waldorf (1983) and Biernacki (1986) in their research on ex-heroin addicts in America.

Avoiding contact with the world of illegal drugs not only helped to avoid the temptations that such associations might pose, it also enabled our interviewees to distance themselves from the drug-using culture which had nurtured and reinforced their pattern of dependent drug use in the first place. However, as we saw, severing their connections with the world of drugs could be difficult to achieve. Successful implementation of the strategy depended on the following: (1) the strength of the individual's ties to those who continued to inhabit that world – for example, if a partner was still using drugs this made disengagement especially difficult; (2) the recovering addict's ability to enter and/or construct an alternative, drug-free world; and (3) the extent to which the world of illegal drugs could be avoided. However, moving away from the drug scene could not only be difficult, it could create problems for the recovering addict as well. For instance, individuals might find it difficult to obtain sufficient money, make friends or occupy their time outside the drug subculture.

As we saw, the development of an alternative set of activities and relationships also appeared to be essential to the process of rehabilitation. First of all, such activities and relationships provided the means by which individuals could occupy their time and replace their former friends. If this does not happen, boredom, loneliness and disillusionment can all too easily draw the individual back into drugs. This risk is likely to be increased to the extent that the drug-using lifestyle continues to retain an appeal for some recovering addicts. However, these new activities and relationships are also vital to the establishment of a new identity. As Biernacki (1986) puts it, they supply the 'identity materials' from which the recovering addict can build and sustain a renewed sense of self. Our study confirms the finding that a scarcity of such materials – for example, through lack of employment or the non-availability of alternative social networks – can be one of the biggest hurdles that recovering addicts have to face.

The alternative lifestyle which these activities and relationships comprised not only provided individuals with an enhanced sense of personal value, it also gave new meaning and purpose to their lives and imbued them with a sense of hope for the future. Paid employment was especially beneficial; it occupied their time constructively, did wonders for their self-esteem and provided a network which could assist in the validation of their new identities. Relationships with non-users were also central to the recovery process; these people provided the necessary social acceptance for the recovering addicts' new status and made it possible for them to participate in the drug-free world. They also provided companionship, which played an important part in preventing loneliness and isolation, thereby neutralising the latter's potential to draw the recovering addicts back into the company of users. As we saw, the more their identities are restored and the more positive and rewarding their drug-free lives become, the more their resistance to returning to drugs is strengthened. In time, their new lifestyle provides them with things that they are simply not prepared to lose. This, in turn, makes a return to using illegal drugs increasingly unlikely.

Methodological issues

Our study was based entirely upon interviews with recovering addicts after their recovery had taken place. There are two potential problems with this sort of research design. Firstly, it relies entirely upon the addicts' own accounts of their recovery and, secondly, all of the data were collected retrospectively. We would like to deal with each of these potential problems in turn, beginning with the study's reliance upon the addicts' own descriptions of their experiences.

We recognise that there are difficulties in treating people's own accounts of their experiences as literal. As we discuss elsewhere, we are also aware that the narratives which interviewees provide in an interview may be designed to serve a variety of purposes (McIntosh and McKeganey 2000b). For example, the past might be described and reinterpreted by individuals in accordance with their current status; in our interviewees' case their new status as former or recovering addicts. Having said that, though, we believe that our interviewees' accounts were reasonably faithful representations of their experiences. In part, our confidence has to do with certain precautions which we took in order to avoid misrepresentation by our respondents. First, we avoided rewarding or privileging any particular set of experiences or views on the part of our interviewees. We made it clear to them that we were as interested in their failures as we were in their successes in relation to coming off drugs; that we were trying to understand the process of recovery from the standpoint of those seeking to come off drugs rather than to reward successful recovery. Second, we did not rely upon the account of any one individual. While it is possible that one or two individuals might have constructed a completely fictional account of their recovery, such fabrications are rather less likely to have been produced by a large number of people and certainly, if they were, you would not expect these fictions to match. By interviewing 70 people it was possible to look at similarities in the individuals' accounts of their recovery and to consider the extent to which these narratives presented a coherent and consistent portrayal of the recovery process. Third, our interviewees were asked to describe the process of recovery from many different angles. They were asked to describe how they came to the decision to cease their drug use, how they sought to develop that commitment within the context of their everyday lives, what impact their drug use and their attempts at recovery had on the people around them and in what ways their recovery was helped or hindered by other people. They were asked to comment on the various drug-misuse services they may have been in contact with during their recovery and to comment in detail on the challenges they faced in overcoming their addiction. While it is possible that an astute and imaginative individual could have provided a coherent set of fictional answers to these questions, we believe it is unlikely that 70 individuals would have been able to do so.

In addition to the precautions which we took to avoid being misled by our interviewees, the nature of the data that we obtained also suggests that their accounts were not simply elaborate fabrications. First, a striking feature of the data was the high level of consistency in our interviewees' descriptions of their recovery and of the significant elements in it. The same themes occurred repeatedly in interviews with different individuals and, in addition, would be referred to frequently by the same person. In short, the major themes were both persistent and consistent. Second, our interviewees' descriptions of the factors involved in their recovery were grounded in their experiences and were consistent with them. In other words, their narratives as a whole exhibited a coherence or completeness; what they had to say connected and made sense.

The second potential problem with our study design is its retrospective nature. A major difficulty with a retrospective approach is that the direction of causality is difficult to assess since there is no way of determining objectively the temporality of different events and processes. This problem is particularly acute in a study like the present one which relied exclusively upon interviewees' own accounts. While our examination of the process of recovery has not, by and large, been about identifying causes so much as describing the various features of the recovery process, there is one aspect of our work where we have entered into the area of causality. This has to do with the role of identity in explaining the individual's decision and commitment to overcome his or her drug addiction. In outlining what seems to us to be the fundamental role of identity in the process of recovery we are not, of course, saying that our interviewees' recovery can be solely explained in terms of the operation of identity. We are also aware that there is a need for research to explore further the role and importance of identity in explaining the recovery from dependent drug use. However, what we hope we have been able to do in this book is to show that underlying many of our interviewees' accounts of their recovery were concerns to do with their identity and that, as a result, identity would seem to be an important and fundamental aspect of their recovery.

Implications for drug services

We would like to conclude this book by looking at what we feel are some of the main implications of our research for those services that are provided to help addicts overcome their drug addiction. Perhaps the first thing to say here is that it is important to apply the addicts' own views of their recovery to our understanding of the operation of those services that are provided to assist them in recovering from their addiction. As we noted in Chapter 6, while it is commonplace within health and social care services more generally to obtain the views of clients and to include those views in the planning and delivery of services, this remains something of a rarity within the drug-misuse field. Over the last few years Drug Action Teams have been formed in many parts of the UK. These teams – comprising senior officials from the health, education, social work and law enforcement arenas – have responsibility for developing a strategic response to drug problems within their own areas. Only rarely have these teams included representation from recovering addicts themselves. In the light of our own research, this would seem to be a serious oversight. The recovering addicts we interviewed showed that they were perfectly capable of providing a considered and distinctive account of their recovery and of the various services that have been provided to help them in that recovery. It is difficult to see the justification for systematically ignoring the voice of recovering addicts in any forum concerned with the planning and delivery of drug-misuse services.

There is a further reason for listening to the views of the addicts themselves which has to do with the centrality of the addict's experience in the recovery process. The addict is central to his or her recovery because the change in status that is entailed in coming off drugs is something that is largely determined by the individual. This is not to say that services have little or no impact on the recovery process but to recognise that, in a fundamental sense, it is the individual who has to change his or her life for recovery to occur. The voice of the recovering addict is, then, not simply one more voice to be added to the existing, and largely professional, chorus of voices involved in planning and providing drug-misuse services but is the one voice above all others that should never be marginalised. The individuals interviewed in our research had much to tell us about the process of recovery from drug addiction. Drug services need to listen to those voices and learn from their experiences.

The second point we would like to make as far as the key implications of our work are concerned is to emphasise the importance of ensuring that drug services are better integrated into the cycle of the drug-using career. Within the UK, and elsewhere, considerable efforts and resources are directed at primary drug prevention, that is, discouraging individuals from starting to use illegal drugs. In contrast, there are relatively few services provided for individuals in the early stages of their drug use. The assumption tends to be made that drug users will have little or no desire to use drug-misuse services until the point at which they have come to experience their drug use as a problem. However, in our view, it would seem unwise to simply stand by and wait for a problematic behaviour to develop before seeking to intervene. Within the context of the development of addictive behaviours, which by their very nature are going to be difficult to change, such a strategy would seem foolhardy. There have been only a small number of attempts to try to influence individuals' drug-using behaviour at an early point in its development. One small project in England, for example, is based upon the recognition that the transition from non-injecting to injecting drug use is a key stage in the career of many addicts and that this transition is very often facilitated by current injectors who will show the naïve injector how to prepare the drugs for injection, what needle and syringe to use and what part of the body to inject into. The project aims, through counselling, to discourage current injectors from initiating non-injecting drug users into the process of injection. The early evaluation of this project has been positive, indicating that it is possible to reduce the incidence of initiation into injecting in this way (Hunt *et al.* 1998, 1999, Stillwell *et al.* 1999). This project is a good example of a service seeking to intervene at an earlier point in the development of a drug-using career and the principle is something that could be valuably extended elsewhere.

The addicts in our research were motivated to come off drugs in large part because they had come to experience a profoundly negative sense of self. The image of themselves they saw reflected back in the lives of the people around them was an image which, in time, they could not accept. Their attempts at constructing a new identity for themselves had both psychological and social dimensions to them. We believe it is essential that staff working in drug-treatment services receive the appropriate training to enable them to support addicts' attempts at reconstructing their identities. However, at the present time, relatively few services will have staff within them who are trained in this way. It is also important to recognise that the work of constructing a non-addict identity involves more than just those services that have an explicit drugs focus. In Chapter 5 we saw how important it was for recovering addicts to break their contact with drug-using acquaintances. The opportunity to move to an area where they were not known as drug addicts, and where they were less likely to meet past drug-using contacts, was extremely beneficial in this regard. It is for this reason that we believe housing staff have a critical role to play in assisting individuals' efforts to remain drug-free. At the present time relatively few housing staff will feel confident in assessing the extent of an addict's recovery and of ranking the housing needs of a recovering addict against those of various other priority groups. Equally, in weighing up the case for relocating a recovering addict, housing staff will also be mindful of the possibility that, if the individual relapses, then relocation may result in the diffusion of drug-misusing behaviours into an area which had not previously had a drug problem. There is likely to be a need, not only to ensure that housing staff have accurate and up-to-date training in drug misuse, but also that such staff are fully supported by professional drug services in those areas in which recovering addicts have been relocated.

Much the same can be said about local employers. If there was one thing that was very clear in the accounts of the recovering addicts interviewed in our research it was that you cannot come off drugs and then sit and do nothing. There has to be an alternative to the drug-using lifestyle that can fill the void in the addicts' lives once drugs have been taken out of the daily round of their activities. Indeed there is probably no surer way of returning to the drug-using lifestyle than sitting alone for hours with nothing to do. There is a clear role here for involving recovering addicts in voluntary activity of various kinds. Ultimately, however, what is needed is for the addict to secure some form of paid employment. However, many employers will be reluctant to employ individuals with a known drug problem for fear that they might relapse and/or cause a range of other problems. Similarly, there are likely to be few employees who will feel positively about such a scheme in their own work place. There will also be those who will say that if anybody is to be helped to secure paid employment then there are other more deserving groups than former addicts. However, at the end of the day, if we are serious about helping addicts to beat their addiction, we will have to supplement our drug-treatment services with much greater provision aimed at rehabilitating the addict once the pains of drug withdrawal have been overcome. To do this we need to ensure that those employers who are courageous enough to provide employment for recovered addicts are supported by appropriately trained staff. Where an employer has provided such a job he or she needs to know that, at the first sign that the individual is not coping, there are services in place to respond immediately to the problem. One approach might be to ensure that drug services provide someone who can 'buddy' the recovering addict in the early stages of his or her employment. Such an initiative is unlikely to be cheap to implement but without increased effort in this direction we are probably not going to benefit fully from the existing input of drug-treatment services.

We also believe that there is a need to develop an environment of constructive challenge within drug-misuse services. In the period following the advent of HIV the fear that injecting drug users might spread HIV infection to the non-drug-using population led to a major shift in the focus of many drug services. Concern with drug addiction itself was somewhat relegated in favour of reducing addicts' HIV-related risk behaviour. Drug services were encouraged to develop user-friendly styles of working and to be as accessible as possible in order to establish and retain contact with drug users over as long a period as possible. With such importance being placed on developing user-friendly services it is perhaps hardly surprising that less emphasis was given to challenging addicts about their behaviour. Our suggestion here is that drug services need both to support the reduction of drug users' risk behaviour and, at the same time, to vigorously address the individuals' need to change. To achieve this, services will need to walk an especially difficult tightrope. On the one hand, they need to do all they can to maintain contact with drug users while, on the other, they need to challenge individuals in a constructive way about the reality of their drug use and drug addiction. As we saw in Chapter 4, addicts' awareness of the impact of their drug use upon their children was a powerful force in promoting their resolve to change. This suggests that drug-misuse services need to encourage and work with addicts in appreciating the impact of their drug use upon the various people around them. Again this is unlikely to be easy to do. Many drug workers will recognise that confronting addicts about the circumstances of their children is a risky business. At worst, it may result in an individual breaking his or her contact with the drug service in question. Premature cessation of drug treatment is, however, an ever-present possibility in any treatment regime and is not in itself a reason for avoiding confronting addicts about the negative aspects of their behaviour.

There is a further reason why it is important for drug-misuse services to focus upon the circumstances of children living within addict house-holds. Quite simply, these children are likely to be at considerable risk. In consequence, while encouraging parents to consider the impact of their drug use upon their children, drug services must, at the same time, maintain a clear and constant watch on the children's welfare. There will be difficult judgements to make here and, while we have tried to show that there is value in encouraging addict parents to focus upon the impact of their drug use on the lives of their children, we would also say that the pre-eminent principle underlying such work has to be a concern for the welfare of the children themselves. There will be occasions when concern for the welfare of a child within an addict household will lead to a decision to remove the child to a place of safety. While such a decision may have a negative effect upon the parents' own recovery, we are clear that the welfare of the child must take precedence over the needs of the adult.

Finally, a major challenge facing those who are planning and deliver-ing drug-misuse services is that of ensuring the closest possible match between the needs of individuals and the content and capacities of the services provided for them. There are two things that will be needed to bring this about. First, we need to ensure that individual drug users are regularly assessed in terms of their needs. These assessments should include the views of drug users themselves. There is a need to establish whether the services that an individual is currently receiving are meeting his or her needs and whether alternative or additional services may be needed. Given that an individual's needs are likely to change over time, such assessments should be undertaken at regular intervals. The second requirement that will be needed to bring about a closer match between individuals' needs and the services provided, is to ensure that we have an appropriate array of services available in each area. At the present time, within many parts of the UK, the level of drug-misuse service provision is woefully inadequate. Clearly, there is no point in assessing the current needs of drug users if there is not a suitable range of services available within each area.

In terms of the implications of our work for drug users themselves, their loved ones and their friends, the one message above all others that we would wish this book to convey is that there is a road back from addiction. We need to learn from the experiences of those addicts who have travelled that road and must do all that we can to support those who are following in their footsteps.

Bibliography

Ball, J.C. and Ross, A. (1991) *The Effectiveness of Methadone Maintenance Treatment*, Berlin: Springer.

Barnard, M. (1999) Forbidden questions: drug-dependent parents and the welfare of their children, *Addiction*, 94(8), pp. 1109–11.

Barnard, M., Forsyth, A. and McKeganey, N. (1996) Levels of drug use among a sample of Scottish schoolchildren, *Drugs: Education, Prevention and Policy*, 3(1), pp. 81–9.

Bauman, K.E. and Ennett, S.T. (1996) On the importance of peer influence for adolescent drug use: commonly neglected considerations, *Addiction*, 91(2), pp. 185–98.

Becker, H. (1963) *Outsiders: Studies in the Sociology of Deviance*, A Free Press Paperback.

Bell, J., Diguisto, E. and Byth, K. (1992) Who should receive methadone maintenance?, *British Journal of Addiction*, 87(5), pp. 689–94.

Bentley, A. and Busuttil, A. (1996) Deaths among drug abusers in south east Scotland (1989–1994), *Medicine Science and the Law*, 36, pp. 231–6.

Bess, B., Janus, S. and Rifkin, A. (1972) Factors in successful narcotics renunciation, *American Journal of Psychiatry*, 128, pp. 861–5.

Biernacki, P. (1986) *Pathways from Heroin Addiction; Recovery Without Treatment*, Philadelphia: Temple University Press.

Blumer, H. (1969) *Symbolic Interactionism; Perspective and Method*, Englewood Cliffs, NJ: Prentice Hall.

Bradley, B.P., Phillips, G., Green, L. and Gossop, M. (1989) Circumstances surrounding the initial lapse to opiate use following detoxification, *British Journal of Psychiatry*, 154, pp. 354–9.

Brill, L. (1972) *The De-Addiction Process*, Springfield, Illinois: Charles C. Thomas.

Christo, G. (1998) A review of reasons for using or not using drugs: commonalities between sociological and clinical perspectives, *Drugs: Education, Prevention and Policy*, 5, pp. 59–72.

Coggans, N. and McKellar, S. (1994) Drug use amongst peers: peer pressure or peer preference, *Drugs: Education, Prevention and Policy*, 1(1), pp. 15–26.

Cummings, C., Gordon, J.R. and Marlatt, G.A. (1980) Relapse: prevention and prediction, in W.R. Miller (ed.), *The Addictive Behaviours: Treatment of Alcoholism, Drug Abuse, Smoking and Obesity*, Oxford: Pergamon Press, pp. 291–321.

Cunningham, J. (1999) Untreated remission from drug use: the predominant pathway, *Addictive Behaviours*, 24(2), pp. 267–70.

Davies, J.B. (1998) *Drugspeak: The Analysis of Drug Discourse*, Harwood Academic Publishers.

Denzin, N.K. (1989) *The Research Act: A Theoretical Introduction To Sociological Methods*, 3rd edn, Englewood Cliffs, NJ: Prentice Hall.

Edwards, G., Oppenheimer, E. and Taylor, C. (1992) Hearing the noise in the system: exploration of textual analysis as a method for studying change in drinking behaviour, *British Journal of Addiction*, 87, pp. 73–81.

Frykholm, B. (1985) The drug career, *Journal of Drug Issues*, 15, pp. 333–46.

Glaser, B. and Strauss, A. (1967) *The Discovery of Grounded Theory*, Chicago: Aldine.

Goffman, E. (1963) *Stigma: Notes On the Management of Spoiled Identity*, Englewood Cliffs, NJ: Prentice Hall.

Gossop, M., Battersby, M. and Strang, J. (1991) Self-detoxification by opiate addicts: a preliminary investigation, *British Journal of Psychiatry*, 159, pp. 208–12.

Gossop, M., Green, L., Phillips, G. and Bradley, B. (1989) Lapse, relapse and survival among opiate addicts after treatment: a prospective follow-up study, *British Journal of Psychiatry*, 154, pp. 348–53.

Gossop, M., Marsden, J., Stewart, D. and Rolfe, A. (2000) Patterns of improvement after methadone treatment: one year follow-up results from the National Treatment Outcome Research Study (NTORS), *Drug and Alcohol Dependence*, 60, pp. 275–86.

Graham, J. and Bowling, B. (1995) *Young People and Crime*, London: Home Office.

Gunne, L.M. and Gronbladh, L. (1981) The Swedish methadone maintenance program – a controlled study, *Drug and Alcohol Dependence*, 7(3), pp. 249–56.

Hall, S.M., Havassy, B.E. and Wasserman, D.A. (1991) Effects of commitment to abstinence: positive moods, stress and coping on relapse to cocaine use, *Journal of Consulting and Clinical Psychology*, 59, pp. 526–32.

Hart, L. and Hunt, N. (1997) Choosers not losers? Drug offers, peer influences and drug decisions amongst 11–16 year olds in West Kent, Invicta Community Care NHS Trust, Maidstone, Kent.

Hawkins, J.D., Catalano, R.F. and Miller, J.Y. (1992) Risk and protective factors for alcohol and other drug problems in adolescence and early adulthood: implications for substance abuse prevention, *Psychological Bulletin*, 112(1), pp. 64–105.

Heather, N. and Stallard, A. (1989) Does the Marlatt model underestimate the importance of conditioned craving in the relapse process? in M. Gossop (ed.), *Relapse and Addictive Behaviour*, London: Routledge, pp. 180–208.

HMSO (1998) *Drug Misuse and The Environment: a Report by the Advisory Council on the Misuse of Drugs*, London: Stationery Office.

Hunt, N., Griffiths, P., Southwell, M., Stillwell, G. and Strang, J. (1999) Preventing and curtailing injecting drug use: opportunities for developing and delivering 'route transition interventions', *Drug: and Alcohol Review*, 18(4), pp. 441–51.

Hunt, N., Stillwell, G., Taylor, C. and Griffiths, P. (1998) Evaluation of a brief intervention to reduce initiation into injecting, *Drugs: Education, Prevention and Policy*, 5(2), pp. 185–93.

Judson, B.A. and Goldstein, A. (1983) Episodes of heroin abuse during maintenance treatment with a stable dosage of acetyl-methadol, *Drug and Alcohol Dependence*, 11, pp. 271–8.

Klingemann, H.K.H. (1992) Coping and maintenance strategies of spontaneous remitters from problem use of alcohol and heroin in Switzerland, *International Journal of the Addictions*, 27, pp. 1359–88.

Klingemann, H. (1994) Environmental influences which promote or impede change in substance behaviour, in G. Edwards and M. Lander (eds), *Addiction: Processes of Change*, Oxford: Oxford University Press.

Kosten, T.R., Rounsville, B.J. and Kleber, H.D. (1986) A 2.5 year follow up of depression, life crises and treatment effects on abstinence among opioid addicts, *Archives of General Psychiatry*, 43, pp. 733–8.

Lehmann, F., Lauzon, P. and Amsel, R. (1993) Methadone maintenance: predictors of outcome in a Canadian milieu, *Journal of Substance Abuse Treatment*, 10, pp. 85–9.

Lloyd, C. (1998) Risk factors for problem drug use: identifying vulnerable groups, *Drugs: Education, Prevention and Policy*, 5(3), pp. 217–32.

Longshore, D., Hsieh, S.C., Danila, B. and Anglin, M.D. (1993) Methadone maintenance and needle syringe sharing, *International Journal of the Addictions*, 28(10), pp. 983–96.

Maddux, J.F. and Desmond, D.P. (1980) New light on the maturing out hypothesis in opioid dependence, *Bulletin on Narcotics*, 32, pp. 15–25.

Maddux, J.F. and Desmond, D.P. (1992) Ten-year follow-up after admission to methadone maintenance, *American Journal of Drug and Alcohol Abuse*, 18(3), pp. 289–303.

Marlatt, G. (1985) Cognitive Factors in the Relapse Process, in G. Marlatt and J. Gordon (eds), *Relapse Prevention: A Self-control Strategy for the Maintenance of Behaviour Change*, New York: Guilford Press.

Marlatt, G.A. and Gordon, J.R. (1985) *Relapse Prevention: Maintenance Strategies in the Treatment of Addictive Behaviours*, New York: Guilford Press.

Mayock, P. (2000) *Choosers or Losers? Influences on Young People's Choices about Drugs in Inner-City Dublin*, The Children's Research Centre, University of Dublin.

McAuliffe, W.E., Feldman, B., Friedman, R., Launer, E., Magnuson, E., Mahoney, C., Santangelo, S., Ward, W. and Weiss, R. (1986) Explaining relapse to opiate addiction following successful completion of treatment, in F.M. Tims and C.G. Leukfield (eds), *Relapse and Recovery in Drug Abuse*, Nida Research Monograph 72, Washington, DC.

McIntosh, J. and McKeganey, N. (2000a) The recovery from dependent drug use: addicts' strategies for reducing the risk of relapse, *Drugs: Education, Prevention and Policy*, 7(2), pp. 179–92.

McIntosh, J. and McKeganey, N. (2000b) Addicts' narratives of recovery from drug use: constructing a non-addict identity, *Social Science and Medicine*, 50, pp. 1501–10.

McIntosh, J. and McKeganey, N. (2001) Identity and recovery from dependent drug use: the addict's perspective, *Drugs: Education, Prevention and Policy*, 8(1), pp. 47–59.

Mead, G.H. (1934) *Mind, Self and Society*, The University of Chicago Press.

Miller, P. and Plant, M. (1996) Drinking, smoking and illicit drug use among 15 and 16 year olds in the United Kingdom, *British Medical Journal*, 313, pp. 394–97.

Myres, M.G. and Brown, S.A. (1990) Coping responses and relapse among adolescent substance abusers, *Journal of Substance Abuse*, 2, pp. 177–89.

Neale, J. (1998) Drug users' views of prescribed methadone, *Drugs: Education, Prevention and Policy*, 5(1), pp. 33–45.

Neale, J. (1999a) Drug users' views of substitute prescribing conditions, *International Journal of Drug Policy*, 10, pp. 247–58.

Neale, J. (1999b) Understanding drug using clients' views of substitute prescribing, *British Journal of Social Work*, 29, pp. 127–45.

Parker, H. and Measham, F. (1994) Changing patterns of illicit drug use amongst 1990s adolescents, *Drugs: Education, Prevention and Policy*, 1(1), pp. 5–14.

Parker, H., Aldridge, J. and Measham, F. (1998) *Illegal Leisure: The Normalization of Adolescent Recreational Drug Use*, London: Routledge.

Prins, E.H. (1994) *Maturing Out: An Empirical Study of Personal Histories and Processes in Hard Drug Addiction*, University of Amsterdam Press.

Prochaska, J.O., DiClemente, C.C. and Norcross, J.C. (1992) In search of how people change; applications to addictive behaviours, *American Psychologist*, 47(9), pp. 1102–14.

Reed, M.D. and Rowntree, P.W. (1997) Peer pressure and adolescent substance use, *Journal of Quantitative Criminology*, 13(2), pp. 143–80.

Rhoads, D. (1983) A longitudinal study of life stress and social support among drug abusers, *International Journal of Addictions*, 18, pp. 195–222.

Robbins, L. (1993) Vietnam veterans' rapid recovery from heroin addiction: a fluke or normal expectation?, *Addiction*, 88, pp. 1041–54.

Riessman, C. (1994) Making sense of marital violence: one woman's narrative, in Riessman, C. (ed.) *Qualitative Studies in Social Work Research*, London: Sage.

Shaffer, H.J. (1992) The psychology of stage change: the transition from addiction to recovery, in J. Lowinson, P. Ruiz, R. Millman and J. Langrod *et al.* (eds), *Substance Abuse: A Comprehensive Textbook*, Williams and Wilkins, pp. 100–5.

Shaffer, H.J. and Jones, S.B. (1989) *Quitting Cocaine: The Struggle Against Impulse*, Lexington, Massachusetts.

Simpson, D.D., Joe, G.W., Lehman, W.E.K. and Sells, S.B. (1986) Addiction careers: etiology, treatment and 12 year follow up outcomes, *The Journal of Drug Issues*, 16(1), pp. 107–21.

Smart, R.G. (1994) Dependence and correlates of change: a review of the literature, in G. Edwards and M. Lader (eds), *Addiction: Processes of Change*, Oxford: Oxford University Press, pp. 79–94.

Sobell, L.C., Cunningham, J.A., Sobell, M.B. and Toneatto, T. (1991) A life span perspective on natural recovery (self change) from alcohol problems, in J.S. Baer, G.A. Marlatt and R.J. McMahon (eds), *Addictive Behaviours Across the Lifespan: Prevention, Treatment and Policy Issues*, Beverly Hills, CA: Sage Publications, pp. 34–66.

Stall, R. and Biernacki, P. (1986) Spontaneous remission from the problematic use of substances: an inductive model derived from a comparative analysis of the alcohol, opiate, tobacco and food/obesity literatures, *The International Journal of The Addictions*, 21(1), 1–23.

Stillwell, G., Hunt, N., Taylor, C. and Griffiths, P. (1999) The modelling of injecting behaviour and initiation into injecting, *Addiction Research*, 7(5), pp. 447–59.

Stimson, G. (1996) Has the United Kingdom averted an epidemic of HIV infection among drug injectors?, *Addiction*, 91(8), pp. 1085–8.

Stimson, G.V. and Oppenheimer, E. (1982) *Heroin Addiction: Treatment and Control in Britain*, London: Tavistock.

Vaillant, G.E. (1983) *The Natural History of Alcoholism*, Cambridge, MA: Harvard University Press.

Waldorf, D. (1983) Natural recovery from opiate addiction: some social-psychological processes of untreated recovery, *Journal of Drug Issues*, 13(2), pp. 237–80.

Waldorf, D. and Biernacki, P. (1979) Natural recovery from heroin addiction: a review of the incidence literature, *Journal of Drug Issues*, 9, pp. 281–9.

Waldorf, D. and Biernacki, P. (1981) The natural recovery from opiate addiction: some preliminary findings, *Journal of Drug Issues*, 11(1), pp. 61–76.

Washton, A.M. (1989) *Cocaine Addiction: Treatment, Recovery and Relapse Prevention*, New York: Norton.

Williams, G. (1984) The genesis of chronic illness: narrative reconstruction, *Sociology of Health and Illness*, 6(2), pp. 175–200.

Winick, C. (1962) Maturing out of narcotic addiction, *Bulletin on Narcotics*, 14, pp. 1–7.

Woody, G.E., McLennan, A.T., Luborsky, L. and O'Brien, C.P. (1995) Psychotherapy in community methadone programs – a validation study, *American Journal of Psychiatry*, 152, pp. 1302–8.

Index